Welcome to Paranor

It was important for me to develop Paranormal Perspectives for those seeking a deeper understanding of the paranormal world. This series is intended for sceptics, believers, and those who have unfathomable experiences and are often frightened by them. These books will help their understanding of what is happening to them.

The Paranormal Perspectives series will explore, in-depth, the encounters, theories, and research into incomprehensible events and how these experiences motivated remarkable individuals to delve deeper and share their extraordinary relationships of the paranormal with the world.

Paranormal Perspectives begins with five books exploring the spectrum of metaphysical events, with insight from the UK's top ghost detective, a licensed clinical psychologist, a retired English professor, a prolific UFO investigator, and a writer specialising in first-hand, personal paranormal encounters.

You, too, may have had a lifetime of unearthly experiences and may wish to add to the series. Please visit 6th-books.com for further information. We look forward to hearing from you.

I hope you enjoy this series as it guides you on your quest and pulls back the veil to shine light into the unknown.

Sleep well,

G L Davies

Author of ***Haunted: Horror of Haverfordwest***

Paranormal Perspectives

One Big Box of 'Paranormal Tricks': From Ghosts to Poltergeists to the Theory of Just One Paranormal Power
by John Fraser

A Jungian Understanding of Transcendent Experiences
by Susan Plunket

Hauntings, Attachments and Ghouls
by G L Davies

Portraits of Alien Encounters Revisited
by Nigel Harry Watson

Where the Spirit Led
by Brad Burkholder

Paranormal Perspectives: Where the Spirit Led

My Improbable Journey into the Coming Age and What I Learned

Paranormal Perspectives: Where the Spirit Led

My Improbable Journey into the Coming Age and What I Learned

Brad Burkholder

6TH
BOOKS

London, UK
Washington, DC, USA

CollectiveInk

First published by Sixth Books, 2025
Sixth Books is an imprint of Collective Ink Ltd.,
Unit 11, Shepperton House, 89 Shepperton Road, London, N1 3DF
office@collectiveinkbooks.com
www.collectiveinkbooks.com
www.6th-books.com

For distributor details and how to order please visit the 'Ordering' section on our website.

ISBN: 978 1 80341 877 3
978 1 80341 884 1 (ebook)
Library of Congress Control Number: 2024911109

A CIP catalogue record for this book is available from the British Library.

Design: Lapiz Digital Services

UK: Printed and bound by CPI Group (UK) Ltd, Croydon, CR0 4YY
Printed in North America by CPI GPS partners

This book is not intended as a substitute for professional medical advice. The reader should consult the appropriate healthcare professional regarding specific needs. All client names used herein are pseudonyms to protect privacy.

Contents

Introduction

Where the Spirit Led is not the story of my mostly boring life. It's the story of an explosive little bit of my life that isn't boring. If you're reading this, it means that my book found a publisher. If enough people like you read this, word of the book will spread through my friends and acquaintances, and most of them will shun me like a leper. Various family members will join them. "Brad Burkholder is a liar," they'll say, "and if he's not a deliberate liar, if he thinks this stuff is true, then he's stark raving mad."

Let them think what they want. I'm willing—no, eager—to undergo a polygraph test or any other reasonable assessment of the truth of any and all statements in this book.

What I have to say to you is about not only what I've learned and *know* to say but also what I'm *compelled* to say. Sometimes when we hear the truth, it resonates inside us in a way that nothing else can. That's our souls telling us it's true. I've heard a resonating truth, followed it and experienced it, and now it's time for me to come forward and share it. I hope you'll give it a chance and see if it resonates for you.

I'll share a few paranormal events that occurred when I was young, then a series of happenings that led me to a remarkably honorable woman who channels Ramoth, an evolved, God-oriented spirit who had many lives on earth but now comes forth from his life as a philosopher in ancient Greece. That opened up for me the world I'd always sought, truths I'd always wanted, meaning in life that I'd always hoped for.

What I have to say deals with God, angels, demons, ghosts, past lives upon past lives and connections among them that give unimagined meaning to history. Along with a few friends, all students of Ramoth, I've dealt with hostile extraterrestrials, even. The story spreads outward in many directions.

I'd like to give special thanks to Yvonne, that "remarkably honorable woman" who, I've often said, is the closest thing to an angel on earth that I've ever known. Because she's a channel, people call her New Age, but she buys into very few New Age concepts. What she does has been around since ancient times. Yvonne began as my spiritual counselor, became my friend, then my sweetheart, then for many years my wife and now is my friend again. Without her, I would have nothing to say. With her gift, she could be a millionaire many times over, but she is remarkably honorable and devoid of greed. How could I not love her?

The spirit Yvonne channels, Ramoth, has consistently given me—as well as all of Yvonne's clients—extraordinary advice since the 1990s. He has channeled information directly to me at times. One Sunday morning in 2001, when my mother suffered a devastating stroke, I needed to contact my brother, but he was away at a beach house he owned. I searched my parents' home for my mother's book of telephone numbers, but it seemed to be nowhere. Desperate, I sat in a chair, tried to collect myself, and mentally asked Ramoth where the book was. Into my mind came the thought to look in the stereo cabinet. What? Who puts a telephone book in a stereo cabinet? But there it lay, on the turntable where Mother played her Herb Alpert albums in the 1960s, when the stereo was new. Ramoth is real.

And so is what I have to say. It will cost me some of the people I know, but maybe it will bring me some new friends. Maybe one of them will be you.

One

Finding Ramoth

What I have to say about my spiritual life begins when I was a very little boy. Once deep in the night I woke to find a beautiful woman sitting on the edge of my bed, looking down at me. She was young, about the age of my mother, but with long golden hair. Just looking at her, I felt that she loved me and that I was safe. Neither of us spoke, but all was well, so I closed my eyes. The next morning I presumed that I'd seen an angel, but I never mentioned the event to my parents. I already knew what would be believed and what wouldn't.

When I was a bit older but long before I started school, one morning I was on my tricycle in the back yard, facing the rear of the house. My mother was behind me hanging clothes to dry. A man walked around the corner of the house and stopped before me.

"Do y'all need any work done around here?" he asked me.

That's an odd question to ask a small child, especially with the mother hardly thirty feet away. I had no answer for the man, so I turned to look at my mom, whose back was toward me. Before calling to her, though, I glanced back at the man. He was gone. Later I realized that he would have to travel nearly thirty feet to disappear around the corner of the house. My actions didn't give him time to do that even if he ran.

We lived in a two-story farmhouse that had belonged to my great-grandparents. Several people had been born there; several people had died there. As I grew older, I often heard my mother speak of "that man" who sometimes came around the corner of the house. She said it was an optical illusion, that it appeared that a man walked a few steps and simply vanished. I was in high school before I thought to question her. I had always assumed that she saw him from the window over the kitchen sink, but no, she always saw him from the kitchen door. That meant that he followed the same path as my own disappearing man.

"What does he wear?" I asked.

"Oh, he looks like a workman—gray pants, gray shirt."

Wow, I thought. "He wears a hat, doesn't he?" I asked.

"A gray ball cap."

I remembered the mystery man—not his face so much, but his clothes—and my mother described him accurately. She'd seen him many times. I'd seen him only once, but he spoke to me. I had told her about the man just after he spoke and vanished, but she dismissed me so completely that at the time of our later conversation, she couldn't recall my ever mentioning him.

One other strange thing happened when I was small. My brother, who was born when I was nearly five, slept in a crib just across from my bed. I woke several different nights to see what looked like a flock of hovering stars above him. In the dim room I could see the wall and ceiling behind the stars as they randomly moved slightly—the way a cluster of gnats might move on a still summer afternoon. I thought they were angels watching over my brother. Once again, there was no use mentioning them to my parents—or anyone else.

The rest of my childhood was less remarkable, except for one event. My parents, my brother, my father's mother and I lived in the farmhouse on ten acres just over a mile from the town of Vinton, Virginia. My parents kept cows and bought a pony for my brother and me about the time I turned six. During late May and early June of 1959, the thought that I was going to break my arm kept passing through my head. I dismissed the idea. I had seen a boy with his arm in a cast and was told simply that he had broken his arm. Not noticing fingers sticking out the end of the cast, I assumed that the remedy for a broken arm was amputation and a prosthetic limb made of concrete. Such a fate for myself seemed impossible in my young mind. But nothing is impossible. I fell off the pony, suffering a compound fracture of the left forearm and dislocation of the elbow. For a few years afterward, my parents treated me like fine crystal—which meant no organized sports. Maybe that's why I took to reading like no other kid I knew. By the summer prior to the third grade, I was reading every magazine I could get my hands on.

When I started school—with my arm still in a sling—I knew a few of my classmates from Sunday school at the Methodist church, but most were strangers. Throughout elementary school I flourished academically, but not socially. The other kids lived in town or in subdivisions; I lived far out the road. They played softball and football; I fed cows and wandered through the pasture behind the house and up the mountain beyond the pasture. They knew as well as I did that there was some sort of divide between us—nothing huge, but something. Still, I did have a few good friends.

Somehow, my brother escaped the divide. Maybe it was simply because he didn't break his arm. Maybe it was because he never conversed with ghosts, never saw stars hover over anyone's bed and never visited with otherworldly women during the night. Maybe it was just because he was the second child and benefitted from more experienced parents.

Later, when I got to college, I would learn that most of my schoolmates and I—in fact, most of my friends and I—simply had different values. My buddies worshipped cars, or seemed to. I spent more time thinking about things I never discussed, things like eternity, the afterlife, our Maker and why we seemed to know nothing logical about those things. Before I could learn anything about values, though, I had to get through high school.

The worst years of my life. Yes, I did have fun, but much of it was a little delinquent. I wandered through confusion as I had once wandered through the pasture. Why do we need pep rallies? Why is school spirit so important? Why does anyone think the prom is a big deal? Why would anyone join a foreign language club? These were just social confusions. Academically, I became a lost cause one minute after a teacher told us that algebra was simplified mathematics. If something is simplified, I think even now, shouldn't it be easy to understand? High school was bad, but not *all* bad. I liked pretty girls, and once in a while one of them liked me too. I discovered that I loved throwing a football, but I wasn't very athletic and didn't like group activities, so I never joined a team. Instead, I hung a tire on a rope and spent hours throwing at it.

During my high school years, like most students, I pondered my future. Obviously, it wouldn't involve math in a big way, and my problems with math ruled out science as well. At one point I thought of becoming a preacher, but I soon came to feel that church—religion, really—was insufficient to its own purpose. I liked writing, but I wasn't sure I would want it as a job. An interesting thing happened in my senior English class, though. That year we studied British literature. I had always preferred literature—especially poetry, oddly enough—to other subjects, even though most of my classmates didn't. When we read Wordsworth's poem with the ghastly title "Ode: Intimations of Immortality from Recollections of Early Childhood," I recognized some of its lines. I *knew* those lines, but when had I ever read or heard them? Similarly, the names of the later English Romantic poets—Keats, Shelley, Byron—were strangely familiar, as if they were friends of the family I hadn't heard from for years. As our studies moved into the latter nineteenth century, the same feeling happened with William Butler Yeats. At the time, I simply wondered and shrugged. It reminded me of the time in the second grade when I saw a television commercial with "William Shakespeare" urging viewers to eat a certain brand of English muffin. I knew who Shakespeare was; I just couldn't remember how I knew.

College came to my rescue—Virginia Western Community College, to be exact. I chose the community college because it was close by, in Roanoke, Virginia, and tuition at the time was $50 per quarter. I didn't know whether I could succeed in college, and it seemed prudent not to gamble much money on me. My parents were footing the bill, and I thought I was making the right decision. The future proved me correct.

I entered scared, believing that college was my one remaining chance to make the rest of my life good. I'd been a mediocre high school student, so I would have to work very hard to be a good college student. However, everything fell into place once I started classes. During my first week the sociology professor said something about sex—and no one sniggered. Maturity was so refreshing, and so new. I had found a comfortable niche.

About that time, I started writing verse—hackneyed stuff, with babbling brooks, rosebuds and other clichés that young, beginning poets somehow think are profound. I showed some of my poems to my English professor, who encouraged me to keep writing and to read as much good poetry as I could. I scoured local bookstores, finding a small collection by a poet named Rod Taylor and also a collection by James Dickey. The most significant poem I discovered, though, had been hiding in my English textbook. It was Yeats's "Sailing to Byzantium." I read it over and over, not understanding it but utterly compelled by what I called an "urgency" in its words. Decades later, the poem still fascinates me, is still urgent. I understand it now and think of it daily. But I no longer read it often. I recite it to myself. And I still write verse.

At Virginia Western a friend suggested that I look into Madison College, a state-supported institution that I knew only as a girls' school. Oh, no, he assured me. It had gone co-ed and even had a football team, yet it was still nearly seventy percent female. Seventy percent female—for that silly reason I was sold on the quaint little college that within a decade would blossom into James Madison University.

In 1973 I transferred to Madison, where I majored in English. There I discovered that the community college had taught me well, that I knew as much as anyone else in my upper-level classes. The English department was full of excellent teachers. I showed my verse to one who seemed approachable, Robin McNallie, who was relatively young and had long, hippyish hair like his students. He thought my writing showed promise and introduced me to Todd Zeiss, who taught creative writing.

Also, during the summer break between my junior and senior years, I met a pretty girl from Vinton who was about to enter Virginia Tech. We would date off and on for the next couple of years and eventually become engaged. Meanwhile, she would excel at Tech, graduating in three years with a double major and a Phi Beta Kappa key.

I owe much of who I am today to Todd Zeiss. I studied poetry composition under him, one-on-one, and progressed considerably in the year and a half that I worked with him. He told me about graduate creative writing programs—which I'd never heard of—and encouraged me to apply to several. I'd already realized that I wanted to teach college English, and specializing in creative writing seemed perfect.

In spring 1975 I graduated with a B.A. from Madison and the following August was living in a co-ed dorm at the University of North Carolina at Greensboro, adjusting to the increased rigors of graduate school and hoping my poetry wouldn't be an embarrassment to me. I studied verse composition under Dr. Robert Watson, who was 28 years my senior and the author of several volumes of poetry. He did just enough teaching to encourage us yet let us find our own way. He never lectured but was always ready to answer a question. I learned much of what I know about teaching creative writing from him.

Also, under Bob, as graduate students called him, I pretty much developed my voice as a poet. Most of my classmates wrote free verse, and I did at times, but I didn't like the randomness of it. In free verse the wisdom, or lack thereof, of the poet determines where within a sequence of words one line ends and another begins. I really wanted to write in rhyme and meter, the way poets did before free verse, but doing that was out of step with the times and surely wouldn't be embraced. I compromised by writing stress verse, sometimes called accentual verse, which set me apart from the other student poets. Most of the poems I've written since have been in stress verse.

As we speak English, some of the syllables we utter are stressed more than others. This is a function of the language; it happens naturally. Some of us can hear those stressed syllables, but many can't. I'm one who can. A poet writing stress verse determines how long his lines will be by deciding how many stressed syllables he will place in each line. The most common line lengths are three stressed syllables or four stressed syllables. For example: "I hate macaroni and cheese" (3 stresses, underlined) or "Yuck—I hate macaroni and cheese" (4 stresses). In stress verse, we don't count the unstressed syllables in a line. Typically, zero, one, two or sometimes three unstressed syllables fall between two stressed syllables, which usually causes a line to sound a little rhythmically different from the lines before and after it. This is similar to the way our Anglo-Saxon ancestors measured lines of poetry, and it sounds somewhat like free verse, but its lines are more consistent in length. It's a happy medium between E.E. Cummings and Robert Frost.

The Master of Fine Arts program at UNC-G took two years to complete. During fall break of my second year, I drove north to Madison College to see my former professors. It was a fortunate visit. As I talked with Dr. Mark Hawthorne, the English department head, he asked if I wanted a teaching job. *Well, yeah.* As easily as that, I was set up to be an instructor of English the following year, the same year the college became James Madison University. I might have been the last person in America to get a college teaching job so casually, and to this day I'm mightily grateful.

After graduating from UNC-G, I spent June and July working with the buildings and grounds crew at my old community college. But during that summer, I got another hint that there is more to this world than we normally admit. I had bought a used motorcycle soon after graduating from high school, and I was about to sell it to help pay for my new start in life. Enjoying the bike one last time, I scooted up a residential street at around thirty-five miles per hour when an old man in a big white station wagon looked straight toward me, failed to see me and pulled out from a stop sign right in front of me. There was so little distance between us. I braked the bike but knew that the next second would hurl me over the car onto the pavement beyond it, dead or ruined for life. Suddenly, and absolutely in defiance of physics, without my doing anything to turn the bike because at the speed I was traveling I *couldn't* turn it, it *did* turn. The bike and I veered ninety degrees to the right, traveled parallel to the station wagon and came to a stop on the street that the car had emerged from. I got off the motorcycle, sat on the curb, thoroughly shaken, and thanked God. I had just taken an impossible ride. Someone didn't want me dead or maimed—at least not yet.

By summer's end my Phi Beta Kappa girlfriend-turned-fiancee and I were married and, with much-appreciated help from my dad and a bank, bought a small house a few blocks from the JMU campus. My first year of teaching was rough. As I learned to teach, the poor students probably learned nothing. I renewed my friendship with Robin McNallie and shared an office with his twin brother, Bruce. I wrote a few poems that I'm still pleased with, and, when Todd Zeiss took a year's leave to work on his own writing, I inherited his creative writing classes.

During that time my wife—let's call her Wife 1—showed some interesting psychic tendencies. In a book I found an experiment in mental telepathy. I was to think of her, then concentrate on an image and finally—this is the hard part—put the whole event out of my mind. The image I concentrated on was Albert Einstein.

"Did you get anything?" I asked.

"I don't think so, just an old guy with crazy hair."

Precisely how I would describe Albert Einstein.

Another time, during a winter cold snap, my wedding band fell off my hand unnoticed. The next morning Wife 1 said: "I think you'll find your ring today. It's on the ground about six inches from a tab top."

That day I did indeed find the wedding band—on the ground about six inches from a tab top.

Once, while visiting the seashore, I woke to find Wife 1 sitting up in bed. The room was dim, not dark, and I clearly saw one Wife 1 from the waist down and two of her from the waist up—one lying on her back asleep and the other sitting up, smiling at me. The smiling Wife 1 then lay down—*into* the sleeping Wife 1. My night's rest was over. I had something to think about.

Back at the university, the department head, Dr. Hawthorne, was highly supportive of me, but from the beginning he had stressed that my one-year contract could be renewed only once, meaning that my stay at JMU would end after the spring 1979 semester. I believed that a second graduate degree would help my chances of sustaining a teaching career, so I applied to Hollins College.

Hollins was a women's college, but its graduate school was co-ed, and it offered a two-semester Master of Arts writing program, unlike UNC-G's Master of Fine Arts program. Studying under the noted poet William Jay Smith with an assist from visiting poet Derek Walcott, who later won the Nobel Prize for literature, I saw my poetry take another step forward. An important factor in that progress was a filmmaking class that taught me to see like a camera and thereby write a bit more vividly. As a bonus, I met the English poet Stephen Spender, who as a young man had met my much-admired William Butler Yeats. At the end of my year at Hollins, I won a filmmaking award and an Academy of American Poets award. I was a well-educated creative writing teacher in need of a job.

I worked briefly driving a delivery truck. Then I began teaching part-time at my old community college, Virginia Western. I had earlier begun a Christmas tree plantation on land my parents inherited from my mother's uncle. I worked for a while as an editor at Nautilus Sports Medical Industries, a company that made equipment for bodybuilders. Later, I became an information officer for Radford University. Then I went back to teaching part-time at Virginia Western, all the while laboring among the Christmas trees, some of which were reaching market size. Early 1987 came, Wife 1 and I split up, neither of us very happy anymore, and I still wrote sporadically. Nothing magical had happened for a long time.

After a brief courtship, I married Wife 2. That was a mistake, especially for her. My income wasn't sufficient. We probably rushed into marriage without knowing one another well enough. For whatever reason, we couldn't find the sort of happiness we needed. Eventually I got on full-time at Virginia Western, and hoping for the best, we had a daughter, the most beautiful baby I ever saw. Having a child is unlikely to bring happiness where happiness is already hard to find, I learned.

While our daughter was a toddler, I wrote a villanelle called "My Daughter Crouching at a Yellow Rose." I deliberately chose a villanelle because it's a difficult rhymed form, and my aim was to craft a poem that could hold its own against other villanelles in the language. In that I hope I succeeded. Because of the repetition built into the form, most villanelles are choppy, with a good many separate sentences. If I may say so myself, the poem below is gracefully lyrical, with long, liquid sentences. Creating the poem was important to me because I believed I would either move out or die young, and in either case it was important to leave my child something no one else could give her.

My Daughter Crouching at a Yellow Rose

My daughter crouching at a yellow rose,
her fingers careful of the danger there,
bending a single flower to her nose,

is unaware that she has struck a pose
or that I've paused from raking grass to stare.
My daughter crouching at a yellow rose

grips the new-mown lawn with grassy toes
and leans her face into the rosy air,
bending a single flower to her nose.

As unselfconscious as the light that glows
in yellow curves along her wispy hair,
my daughter crouching at a yellow rose

breathes deeply once and then abruptly flows
across the lawn, with no time left to spare
bending a single flower to her nose.

By moments such as this a lifetime grows,
yet moments stream away and with them bear
my daughter crouching at a yellow rose,
bending a single flower to her nose.

Meanwhile, at the college I worked with a lady who was very nice but also was what I call an energy vampire—one of three such people I've known. Just being around her made my knees weak. If I could, I sat while in her presence. As she talked to me, the energy in my body literally drained away, and I felt that if I stayed around her long enough, I would fall asleep. Nevertheless, she was a New Age-type person, often going to spiritual meetings, taking tai chi classes, talking about feng shui and so on.

Then one Monday morning she was different. I didn't feel my energy draining. Her face was animated, her eyes sparkling. She had seen a shaman who performed soul retrieval for her. After several days, when I was convinced that she really was changed, I asked for the shaman's phone number.

The shaman had been in town only for the weekend and had returned home to Michigan but could do the work from anywhere. My colleague advised me to ask him for soul retrieval, chakra cleansing, aural cleansing and the identity of my animal spirit guide. Souls, chakras and auras I believed in, but animal spirit guides—hmm. I phoned the shaman, who refused to use the word "shaman," saying instead that he "journeyed." (I learned later that true shamans never use that word to describe themselves.) He promised to journey for me and do the things I asked at 11:00 on a certain morning. I said I would be teaching at that time. Not a problem, he assured me.

At the appointed time I was indeed delivering a long-forgotten lecture to a class of about 25 students. I recall sweating a bit, becoming slightly cloudy-headed and feeling my throat tighten, but I taught right through it.

That afternoon, as pre-arranged, I telephoned the journeyer. He explained that he had started by lying on the floor of his house while his wife beat a drum rhythmically to help him slip into a trance. Then he and his own animal spirit guide had traveled to me. He had retrieved three lost parts of my soul, he said, and was able to describe how old I was when I lost each and under what circumstances it happened. I recognized two of the three incidents. As for my chakras, he said they were full of gunk that had to be wiped away with a feather. Also, he had removed armor plating from around my heart, congestion from my eyes and lungs and some sort of constriction from around my throat. All that for a hundred bucks.

The effects were real. I felt lighter, younger, more alive. For years previously, whenever I tried to fill my lungs to capacity, I coughed; since that day filling my lungs has never made me cough. Strange to say, I had always felt intimidated by waitresses and cashiers; since that day I have not, and I'm much more at ease with strangers. People remarked that my eyes seemed brighter. One man said I seemed taller. Most of these people had no idea that I had hired a shaman. Even in this enlightened age, it isn't the sort of thing one runs through the halls of a college shouting about.

And about that animal spirit guide: the shaman identified him as a male great horned owl and told me his very exotic name, which I was never to divulge lest someone with bad intent call him and use him against me. Furthermore, the shaman predicted that I would soon have some interaction with a great horned owl.

And I did. A few nights later, I woke feeling a feather tickling my face. Then I found an owl feather on the floor of my house. Over a year later, while staying with my brother and sister-in-law, as we sat outside one evening I asked if they ever heard owls. They said no. Moments afterward, a great horned owl began hooting.

I think it's important to strive for maturity and to live with as much maturity as possible. Maturity has been a goal of mine for the last twenty-odd years. Many people reading my words would say that they show the opposite, that I'm spinning an absurd, childish daydream or that I'm deluded. I have no control over what others think—words are weak against unbelievers. All I can say, feebly, is that life presents itself differently to different people depending on our individual karma and with what purpose we entered this world.

I have no words of criticism against either of my first two wives. About myself I will state this: I am eccentric, often distant and in those days less mature, more angry and capable of reactivity. Sometimes my words were sharp. Young people are still learning how to be human. In both marriages something we didn't understand brought us together, ran its course and drove us apart. In time, I would learn a good bit about that force. However, it would take two more women to bring that learning to light.

I filed for divorce in summer 1996. A new relationship came to me, this one overpowering and obsessive. I easily convinced myself that she was the most beautiful thing I had ever seen and the most valuable commodity in the entire world. I would have battled Goliath for her. Little did I know that because of her—and with her—I was about to learn the secret that has allowed virtually everything in my life to make sense.

Her part in that secret, however, made her uncomfortable, whereas I was—and obviously am—willing to tell people about it. But to honor her privacy, I won't divulge her name. She was the Woman.

The Woman was not nearly as obsessed with me as I with her. She did love me, I think, but she found me suffocating. During our three years or so together, I wrote more verse than in any previous three years of my life. I even wrote two full length two-act plays. The biggest problem I had with her was that she was an elusive sort, a born flirt whom I never quite trusted. Sometimes she didn't want to see me. Once she asked me never to call again. My heart was in continual turmoil. But when things were good, I was in absolute bliss.

For reasons I didn't understand, I couldn't shake her out of my mind. Whatever I did, her face hovered in front of me. When I thought about anything, I thought about her as well. She was my last thought as I fell asleep and my first thought as I woke. I was drowning in the idea of her, and somehow that seemed like a good thing. During that time I wrote this little poem, which I think very well expresses the spell I was under, how I felt and how pathetic I was without even acknowledging it:

Siren

We have lingered in the chambers of the sea
By sea-girls wreathed with seaweed red and brown
Till human voices wake us, and we drown.

—T.S. Eliot

Because her eyes are deep, clear water
on a gemstone bed
and I'm adrift upon their tide,

because I know the pull
of every motion of her fingers
as she ebbs away,

because she's in my sleep
and on my waking like the sun
and in my work like need,

to her song I give my words.
This plunge is not to dread.
It's why a man would want to live.

In mythology a siren inevitably lures a sailor to his death. The speaker in the poem would rather die than turn away from the siren. As teenagers in my day would say: "This guy's got it bad."

In March 1997 I was, indeed, miserably drowning in the sea of love when who should come to my rescue but the very lady who had put me in contact with the shaman a year earlier. She had been seeing a woman—a trance channel—who came into town every two weeks and gave readings at a New Age bookstore. I called for an appointment.

A trance channel is a person who, like a shaman, goes into a meditative trance and allows a spirit to speak through him—

or her—somewhat like the ancient Greek oracles. My best knowledge of trance channels came through my knowledge of my favorite poet, William Butler Yeats, whose wife had channeled to him many notebooks' worth of information.

My life was about to change.

Two

Finding Myself

Yvonne (pronounced E-VON) sat in a wooden rocking chair in a little room above a New Age bookstore in an old section of Roanoke, on just the sort of mellow, vintage street where a New Age bookstore belonged. She was about my age, with a ready smile, brown eyes and short black hair. Her makeup looked heavy in an old-fashioned way, and her dress with its big floral print looked like it should be on her mother, not her. I had no idea I was meeting the most important person of my life. (Also, within a few years she gave up the matronly look and became—well, perfect.)

I had booked a half-hour session and had brought a list of questions. She put me at ease, explaining that for eight years she had channeled Ramoth (pronounced RAY-MOTH, with only slightly more emphasis on the first syllable). Ramoth is a kind, wise spirit who sees our world from a better perspective than we can achieve here on earth. Yvonne taped all sessions and gave the tapes to her clients so they could review them and contemplate Ramoth's words. She had me sit on a chair facing her and turned on the tape recorder.

It didn't work. The batteries were dead.

"I'll get some at the store next door," I said, starting for the door.

"Wait." Yvonne reached for her pocketbook.

"I've got it," I said over my shoulder.

When I returned, Yvonne seemed flustered that I would buy her two AA batteries, but to me, it was just the right thing to do.

The session started. Yvonne leaned back in the rocker, closed her eyes and inhaled sharply three times. Then her head began swaying gently from side to side. When Ramoth spoke, it was with Yvonne's voice but with greater volume than I'd heard from her, and the rhythm of his wording was different.

"Many doors you have tried, many paths, but the happiness you seek has eluded you," he said. "Question?"

I had read that to avoid being misled or even victimized, one should always ask a channeled spirit if he/she is of God. If the answer is no, vague or dismissive, the session needs to end. In fact, the Apostle John says precisely that in the opening sentence of Chapter 4 of his first letter, in the New Testament. I refer to the King James Version, but I have also read a direct translation from the Greek version of the New Testament, in which John refers to "inspired speech"—channeling. Come to think of it, if not through channeling, how is one to speak to spirits?

Ramoth was indeed of God, he said, and even spoke of Jesus.

"Did He really exist?" I asked.

"Yes."

"Was He the Son of God?"

"Yes."

Ramoth knew facts about me and my personal history that Yvonne couldn't possibly have known. He had answers about the Woman, who was the reason I had come to him. Her feelings for me were not as strong as mine for her. She was torn between me and a previous relationship. She needed time to make decisions about her life. This wasn't exactly what I wanted to hear, but it was helpful.

I asked about past lives. Raymoth said that I had lived many times in Europe. He saw me centuries ago in a churchyard. I was a 38-year-old priest, very sad because I had no children. He was dropping me a hint—and now I'm passing it along. More about the priest later.

I left that first session already a changed man. I was still concerned about the relationship with the Woman, but something wondrous had happened. The door to existence beyond our five senses had opened a crack, and I had peeked through it. I wanted more. Every paranormal event in my life had been leading to this, and big answers were in the offing. Maybe life could make sense after all. I was hooked.

After that, I booked a full hour with Yvonne every time she was in town—usually every other Saturday. During my second reading, the bomb went boom.

"Why do I think she's the most beautiful woman in the world?" I asked.

"Because she touches your heart, and she did before," Ramoth said.

"In a past life?"

"Yes."

Then a thought hit me. Maybe Ramoth put it in my mind.

"Were we in Ireland?"

"Yes."

"Was she an actress?"

"Yes."

"Was I a poet?"

"Yes."

"Was she Maud Gonne?"

"Yes."

My voice dropped to little above a whisper.

"Was I William Butler Yeats?"

"Yes."

I immediately broke into tears.

"I was William Butler Yeats?" I sobbed. "How can that be?"

"How can it not be?" asked Ramoth.

"He's always been my favorite poet," I choked.

"Now you know why."

Yeah. Now I knew why.

When information like that comes, it's as if a dam bursts inside the soul. Suddenly, so much, so very much makes sense. It's as if you knew it all along but had forgotten it, and the knowledge just explodes into your consciousness. I knew it was true from my soul outward. Although decades have passed since that moment of revelation, I have never doubted for a moment that I was Yeats. I carry him inside me. He speaks through me. No, I'm not the poet he was, but when I write a poem, he's with me.

Since that one "yes" from Ramoth, I've understood the urgency of "Sailing to Byzantium," the Yeats poem that so intrigued me as a college freshman. As I read that poem through the years, a part of me was trying to tell something to another part of me. Finally, I got the message.

Delusions of grandeur? Well, I probably can't convince a skeptic otherwise, but let's remember that it's William Butler Yeats we're discussing here, not Julius Caesar. Go to your local shopping mall and ask the first hundred people you see to identify Yeats. It would surprise me if as many as ten even know the name. He might be a big fish in my little poet bowl, but most deluded people prefer big fish in big bowls.

People who know anything about Yeats are aware that he spent his adult life tortured by a troubled relationship with Maud Gonne, a wealthy woman who did whatever she wanted, came and went as it pleased her and vexed her poet suitor for over 50 years. Ramoth told me that he didn't want me to follow Yeats's pattern, that my heart could be scarred by such a relationship, as Yeats's was. But if anything, I wanted the Woman more, not less.

On my way home from the reading, shaken, I stopped by my parents' house. Against my better judgment, but very excited, I played the important section of the tape for my mother. Her response baffled me. "Who was I?" she asked. I didn't know—yet. Later, I realized that she probably didn't know who Yeats was. My father arrived a few minutes later, and he did know that Yeats was a poet, but he thought the man had lived centuries ago and had died young. (Yeats was born in 1865 and died in 1939 at 73.)

Moments later, exhausted, I fell asleep on the couch in my parents' living room. When I woke, my dad was standing over me, looking down at me. But then—he just dissolved. I sat up to find him asleep in his favorite chair, a few feet away. A little magic had come back.

Two weeks later the Woman herself booked a reading and afterward sent me this email: "Ramoth is real." In her session she had mentioned a man she was seeing. "Yes, the poet," Ramoth said.

I too had a reading that day, and much to ask about. In the past I had idly noted that the Woman's last name rhymed with "Gonne." But in the days leading up to that third session, I had pondered the fact that Yeats and I were not the only two poets bedeviled by such a woman with such a name. In the early 1800s a young Englishman named John Keats had experienced a painful relationship with one Fanny Brawne. "Keats" and "Yeats" look alike but don't actually rhyme—"Keats" being pronounced "Keets" and "Yeats" being pronounced "Yates." However, their ladies' surnames did rhyme, and they both rhymed with the name of the Woman.

I asked Ramoth if Yeats and Gonne were reincarnations of Keats and Brawne. Indeed they were, he told me. I was unsurprised, for I had already formed the hypothesis, yet I was gratified and flattered. Since college, I had considered John Keats my second favorite poet, and a very close second. Perhaps it was simply that Yeats was more modern and used language closer to my own. Still, since undergraduate school I had admired Keats's use of imagery above that of any poet, and in graduate school I once told a friend that when I wrote verse, it seemed that Keats was across the table from me, setting a standard, being the ideal.

These days I don't rank one above the other. Keats might have been the more gifted of the two, but he died at 25. I think one of the greatest poems in English is his "Ode on a Grecian Urn."

William Faulkner, the Nobel Prize-winning novelist, wrote that it was worth "any number of old ladies." High praise, indeed. I don't know of a more beautiful, more perfect poem than "To Autumn," another of his odes. Given a long life, what might he have written?

This is not to downplay the importance of Yeats. Aside from "Sailing to Byzantium," he wrote many fine lyrics. "The Wild Swans at Coole" is exquisite. "Among School Children" ends transcendently. "Leda and the Swan" is a big, big statement in a small package—but more about that later. The man deserved his Nobel Prize.

Having Keats and Fanny in the mix, in the short term, only made me worship the Woman more. Those few of us who study English-language poetry and poets, including myself at the time, often think fondly of Fanny while possibly thinking of Maud as an antagonist. This might be only because Yeats obsessed over Maud for 52 years, yet Keats and Fanny knew each other only a short time due to his early death from tuberculosis. Also, I knew of Fanny only through words. I had seen plenty of photographs of Yeats and Maud, and frankly, I've never found Maud very attractive. I certainly thought the Woman was, though, and one day when we were together in a bookstore, she came to me with a slender volume of Keats's poems open to a full-page portrait of Fanny Brawne. I was stunned. Keats's girl had blue eyes and darker hair, and my girl had brown eyes and lighter hair, but other than those features and the fashion changes of 170 years, they were one and the same. A feature I'd found charming in the Woman was that her philtrum—the little channel that runs from between the nostrils to the upper lip—was just a little slanted. Find a picture of Fanny Brawne and look at hers. It's just a little slanted.

A concern that Ramoth expressed to me was that Keats and Yeats both pestered me psychically, especially now that the Woman was in my life. He said that my brain was full of detrimental chatter. I knew what he meant. My mind was never like a calm, glassy lake. It churned. I was sharing it with two other guys, he told me, and we all three were crazy for the same woman. Something needed to be done.

First he wanted me to meditate daily. He gave me specific instructions. I was to sit or even lie comfortably and close my eyes. Then, I was to make three important statements, either spoken or mentally: "I surround myself with God's white light"; "I demand that only that which is of God and light may enter my space"; and "I demand in the name of God and light that all negativity leave my space at once." Then I was to concentrate on breathing rhythmically, trying to keep random thoughts from intruding. If I fell asleep, no harm was done, he assured me. (In fact, the Dalai Lama has said that sleep is the best form of meditation.)

In addition, Ramoth suggested to Yvonne—in her thoughts—that she take me on a guided regression, something that she normally didn't do. Yvonne generally disliked regressions, especially past-life regressions, because they frequently caused people to relive traumatic events, particularly death, and could leave a person worse off than before. She trusted Ramoth to guide her as she guided me, if I was sure that I wanted the regression. Of course I was sure.

We sat facing one another, as if for a reading. Yvonne soothingly guided me into a meditative state, possibly a mildly hypnotic state. I believe that she could see in her mind the same images I saw in mine. She had me become myself as a little boy. She asked where I was. The kitchen. What did I see? My mother cooking, her back to me. I could actually smell turnip greens, kale or something like that in boiling water. We went into another room, where I found myself in a playpen. My father, very young, was looking down at me. He had on a hat and coat and was about to leave, maybe for work. Next I saw my father's mother, who lived with us. I realized that she was afraid, not of anything in particular, more that she lived in a state of dread. Then I saw my mother's father, and we locked eyes. In his eyes I saw something, knew something that surprised me. He loved me more than the others did, more than anyone did. I had never realized that.

My grandfather drifted away, and my grandmother reappeared. I was no longer a child but a man. As we looked at each other, I wanted her fear to leave. Bit by bit it did. As I watched, her face changed, showed happiness, freedom. In life, she had had spots on her face. As her expression changed, the spots disappeared. She faded away, and I found myself outdoors, next to a small stream. On the stream's bank stood a gnarled, limbless dead tree. Yvonne instructed me to look closer. What I had taken for a tree was actually my grandfather, miserably contorted. What I had seen as bark was actually a dirty overcoat twisted around him. As I looked, my grandfather untwisted, became himself as once he had been in life, a tall, straight man.

Yvonne—or Ramoth, perhaps—said: "You have healed your grandparents. Now heal yourself. Before you stand two men whom you have been."

There they were, a short man on the left and a tall man on the right—Keats and Yeats.

Conceptually, it is one thing to heal a person of something negative—spots on the face, fear, a twisted body. But how does one heal love? Granted, the love in question was obsessive and therefore unhealthy, but it was still love. I don't think any of the three of us was ready to give it up. No, healing didn't happen for John, William or Brad that day.

On the other hand, not only did my deceased grandparents gain something from the session, but maybe I did too. My mind might have become a little less crowded, my meditations a little calmer, which might have led to the next step.

Probably at least partly with healing in mind—although that idea has occurred to me only recently—Ramoth soon had me experimenting with automatic writing. My best knowledge of automatic writing came mostly through something I knew from Yeats's biography. After having a final marriage proposal to Maud Gonne refused, at age 52, Yeats married a woman of 26, Georgie Hyde-Lees. On their honeymoon, to rouse him out of depression(!), Georgie experimented with automatic writing. This was sure to get the old guy's attention. Yeats had long been interested in arcane sciences and the occult, joining groups of similar-minded people, pondering reincarnation, studying astrology and other forms of divination, attending séances—in short, being a little like myself. One difference, I *believe,* is that I have always been a bit more God-oriented and more wary of demonic interference. However, this belief derives from an assumption about another person's inner self—which is always arrogant and unfair.

Apparently, Georgie's attempt at automatic writing followed the usual format: sit at a table or desk with paper before you and writing instrument in hand, sink into a meditative state, allowing your hand to draw circular shapes on the paper, and, just maybe, a spirit will begin directing your hand to write information. Georgie was successful; Yeats, redirected, snapped out of his honeymoon depression. And, he demanded more and more automatic writing sessions during which he asked questions of the spirit. Eventually, the poor girl wore out from all that writing.

Since automatic writing is a type of channeling, Georgie made an easy transition to trance channeling. All she had to do was fall asleep and talk. Yeats, conversing with his spirits just as I did with Ramoth, filled numerous notebooks with information before the channeling sessions just—ended. Yeats summarized his learnings in a book titled *A Vision,* which has been roundly criticized and poo-pooed by nearly everyone who has read it. For many scholars, it's the most embarrassing and inexplicable aspect of Yeats's life. Yeats himself admitted that not all of the channeled information came from the same spirit and that some of the spirits contradicted others. Personally, I find the book interesting but full of baloney.

Naturally, I discussed Yeats's spiritual work with Ramoth. No, Georgie Yeats did not channel Ramoth, and no, Yvonne was not the reincarnation of Georgie. The spirits informing Yeats were not highly evolved, Ramoth said. Some of them enjoyed teasing and misinforming him.

The danger of contacting irresponsible or even demonic spirits always exists when channeling. Remember the Apostle John's statement at the beginning of Chapter 4 of his first letter. Always demand to know if the spirit comes from God. Remember that it is vital to surround oneself with light, demand that only that which is of God come forth and demand in God's name that all negativity be gone. While on the subject, note that many people naively open doorways for evil entities by playing with spirit boards, also called Ouija boards. Yvonne and I have experimented with these boards together, always with bad results, causing us to have to cleanse our space with prayer and burning sage and to destroy the board by burning it. One must be careful. I think the Yeatses were not.

When Raymoth asked me to try automatic writing, he had me meditate with a notebook in my lap and a pen nearby. After meditating, I would write whatever came to mind. At first I got a little information, some of it interesting or moderately useful. After a while I tried creating a poem through automatic writing. On that day I meditated with Ravel's *Bolero* quietly playing. When I began writing, the verse came effortlessly and quickly. The poem's content was related to the music, or more accurately my concept of the music. I titled the poem "Ravel's *Bolero*," and I don't recall making any revisions to it. I channeled it from somewhere, maybe my higher self (whatever that is, exactly), maybe from Keats or Yeats or even some other dead poet.

Ravel's *Bolero*

The eye follows a great bird soaring
in a warm sky, falls to a mountain peak,
its wooded slopes departing left and right,
eases down the trunk of a ragged pine
in the foreground, down to the forest floor, where
the lovers lie propped against a fallen log.
Their lips pull apart, he brushes hair
from her face, their bare feet rub together,
again lips walk on lips, hands rove
sides and backs, eyes open to eyes.
Their breath is music. It marches. The low strings
thrum. The sun shines on the ragged pine,
the mountain breathes in green, and in the sky
a single bird is soaring, soaring still.

One might or might not like the poem. In fact, the poem might or might not be any good. Nevertheless, it came without struggle, making it unlike any poem I had written previously.

Before I would get the Woman out of my system, I would eventually write two full length two-act plays. I wrote the first, *A Rose in a Bottle,* in eleven days. It came effortlessly, partly or completely channeled, I believe. I had no outline or preconceived storyline. I had no plan for how it would end until I got far enough into the play that, knowing what I did about plot-building, I could foresee where the events were inevitably leading. I seemed to be writing at least almost automatically. The play is about Yeats's death. Maud Gonne is a major character, of course.

The second play is to me more impressive. It was definitely channeled, and I know by whom. That story is for another page, though.

Automatic writing told me about another woman who would come into my life. She would be "no lover of cities." I would see her in a black coat with shining shoes. Needless to say, for months I glanced down at the shoes of every woman I saw in a black coat.

Three

Students and Victims

As much as the Woman occupied my life, my sessions with Ramoth were not all about her. I wanted answers to the big questions, the questions philosophers and theologians ask. Ramoth taught me—and others as well—that the purpose of life is to grow and to change, to evolve. We do this by learning life's lessons and acting upon what we learn.

Indeed, Ramoth said, there are two types of people—students and victims. All people make mistakes, but students of life learn from their mistakes and grow from them, becoming wiser and less likely to make the same mistake again. We are on earth to learn. Mistakes and frustrations large and small are part of life and are meant to be used as stepping stones to wisdom, to the evolution of our souls. Victims, on the other hand, fail to learn from mistakes. Instead, they make the same mistakes again. Yeats was a victim, Ramoth told me, adding that he would prefer that I become a student. Eventually it occurred to me that he was gently telling me I was being a bone-headed victim myself.

A good starting point for becoming a student of life is to realize—fully realize—that the same old pattern will produce the same old result. A person jumping out of a bad relationship who then chooses a new partner similar to the old partner is simply remaking the old relationship, thus becoming a victim of life. A person aware enough to consider why the old relationship didn't work and to seek a different type of partner—someone with whom to make a different type of relationship—is a student of life and is building a better life, learning, growing, becoming a better version of self. Life's purpose is to thrive, not to wither.

I once told Ramoth that I wanted to know what he knew, to be more like him. In time such a thing is possible, he said. It comes through being a student, which brings about the evolution of the soul itself. He wants to become like the Apostle John, whom he works with. John is working to become more like Jesus. Jesus Himself is learning and growing.

Creation is eternal. Your life and mine are God's creations, even though we have free will and the ability to mess them up royally. Our souls are little bits of God. God experiences our world through us. When we create, He feels it. When we destroy needlessly, He feels that too. When we help a person in need, we help a little bit of God, and He is happy. When we slam a door in someone's face, we slam it in God's face. When we help ourselves grow, we help God and His universe. To help ourselves, we need to be students of life, to learn from our mistakes and from our successes. They both can be excellent teachers.

Karma is a law of life, at least for all of us who visit earth. It's what we make while we're busy doing other things. The preacher who becomes a multi-millionaire from the donations of his flock instead of using that money to clothe the poor is creating unfortunate karma, just like the man who enters a bank with a submachine gun or the online scammer who wipes out the life savings of a retiree. On the other hand, I know a man who set up a small foundation to send motorcycles to doctors in remote parts of Africa so they could quickly get from one village to another and save lives. He created some karma too, but of a whole different type.

Karma is what balances the scales. It's why we can't live just one life on earth and be done with it. It is fair compensation for each of our actions. Take a dollar from a man, and you will owe him a dollar. Give a dollar, and someday, maybe in a different life, a dollar will come to you. Obviously, we don't usually understand the karma that passes from life to life, but our souls do, and as we retire that karma, we uncomplicate our lives, we purify our souls, we shed the effects of self-victimization, we grow and evolve.

Keats, Yeats and I, Fanny, Maud and the Woman were all involved in some tangled web of karma that might have stretched back thousands of years and hundreds of lives. For some reason Ramoth, who is of God and acts under God, intervened on my behalf. If I have, with his help, retired the painful karma that bound us together, then maybe that alone has made my life worthwhile.

In the minute after I learned that I had once been Yeats, while I tried to compose myself, Ramoth asked: "Why do you believe you have been given this information?"

I could hardly think. I heard myself say: "For a great spiritual purpose."

"Yes," he said.

Very early in my studies under Ramoth, he recommended that I read the Book of Revelation. I had read Revelation previously, but I read it again, several times, read it without preconceptions and critically, as an English professor should. To this day it reminds me of a puzzle with a piece or two missing. But twenty years after my first Ramoth-inspired reading, I developed a few thoughts about Revelation. Ramoth supported them. Here goes.

It is not the Book of Prophesy; it is the Book of Revelation, and the word "revelation" is not plural. Maybe I'm looking too closely at semantics, but the wording implies that one truth is being revealed—a truth, not a prophesy. Throughout the course of history, have the four horsemen not ridden time and time again? Have we not experienced war time and time again? Have mothers not despaired for their babies time and time again? Have victims not huddled, praying for deliverance, time and time again? Does the cycle not repeat? Could Revelation be a picture of how the human race comports itself through the vastness of time? Is it a pattern of behavior that's being revealed? We have learned to make deadlier weapons, but have we learned to live in harmony?

Destructive patterns. If an individual continues to follow a destructive pattern, suffering consequences time and again, according to Ramoth's definition that individual is a victim. Ultimately, who makes that person a victim? Himself. But if he recognizes that his pattern isn't working and changes it, he will cease to suffer the same old consequence. He is now a student. He has changed the pattern that kept him stagnated and can now take a big step forward on the path of life. He has evolved.

Perhaps Revelation shows something different to everyone who reads it without prejudice. Perhaps we should all read it, read it without dread. I'm convinced that it doesn't reveal something terrible about the future but something terrible about the present—and the past. We too seldom use it, yet we have the power to change the future.

Ramoth has told me that he can foresee the future on earth fairly accurately, but only for about two years. That's because the future is shaped by our free will. Ramoth's view of the future is based on conditions as they currently exist. If one of us, some of us, all of us change the pattern we are currently in, we create a ripple small or large within the present and possibly across the globe, maybe even across the universe.

Even God does not know every aspect of the future, Ramoth said. If He did, we likely couldn't have free will, could we? Besides, God is a creator, *the Creator*, and perhaps the manner in which we exist in His image is that in a more limited way we are creators too. Every one of us engages in creativity. It brings delight into life. The impetus to create is to observe our efforts taking shape, to see our creation evolve, to follow where our work leads. The pleasure is largely in the process. We think we know what our creation will be like, but usually the outcome brings a surprise, and sometimes the surprise is delightful.

Always knowing the result of our efforts would be like always reading the final chapter of a book first.

Earlier, I proposed that the Book of Revelation is not prophesy. But what is prophesy? Many people don't believe in prophesy because most prophesied events don't occur. Maybe that's the point. Suppose we are told by a prophet that the world will end next Thursday, no matter what we do. How does that knowledge help us? What can it do other than ruin the next few days? (Oh, yes, we can spend our last days ardently praying for forgiveness and repenting, but praying and repenting under duress surely falls into the category of too little, too late, too hypocritical.) The Book of Jonah can be read as a lesson on the nature of prophesy.

In this short Old Testament book, God tells Jonah to travel to Nineveh and tell the people there that because of their evil He will destroy the city and the people in it. Jonah knows that doing so will make him appear foolish; besides, the rough crowd in Nineveh is likely to kill him. Seeking escape, he books passage on a ship crossing the Mediterranean. On board are many men from many cultures worshipping many gods. Well out to sea, Jonah sleeps soundly during a horrendous storm that threatens to sink the vessel. A man wakes him, saying that everyone is about to die and that all are convinced that the storm is the result of someone on board having offended a god. Jonah pleads guilty and bravely offers to be thrown overboard. His shipmates oblige. Fortunately for him, God has a ride waiting.

Back on shore, Jonah probably smells awful—just imagine the strength of whale breath. God asks if he is ready to go to Nineveh. Jonah goes. He preaches the prophecy, and the Nineveh rowdies let him live. Curious to see the city's destruction, Jonah builds a shelter on a high spot with a good view, and there he dwells for so long that a plant grows from the ground and shades his temporary home. Nothing happens. Eventually God comes to Jonah with words something like these:

"Angry with me, huh?"

"Yes. You said You would destroy the city."

"But your prophesy worked. Some of the people heeded your words. They changed. For the sake of those good people I will spare the rest."

So, indeed, prophesy is not a statement of what definitely will happen but a warning of what will happen if the present pattern prevails. Make a change, change the pattern, change the outcome. Or, maintain the status quo and, in the case of Nineveh, be destroyed. Nineveh changed a little, though, just enough to avert the prophesied destruction. Once again, we see the choice to be a student or to be a victim. Students keep dire prophesies from coming true.

Some people see the Book of Jonah as a true account, and others see it as a parable. Either way, it shows how a prophesy can be a successful effort from the spiritual world to bring a positive change in the material world—a good creation, if you will. A great work of literature from the ancient world shows what happens when people confronted with prophesy fail to handle it with insight.

Sophocles wrote *Oedipus Rex* at about 500 BCE. Let's summarize not just the play but also the legend it's based on. The king and queen of Thebes have a baby boy, an heir to the throne. The queen visits an oracle to learn about her son's future. The oracle prophesizes that the son will murder his father, marry his mother and sire children with her. Bad news, indeed. The horrified parents have a choice that they overlook, with dire consequences. They could decide to be the best parents possible so as to keep the horrifying events from occurring. Consider: in a nurturing, functional household, how often do sons kill their fathers? And isn't it even less likely that a son would *marry* his mother and have children with her? Marriage implies consent, doesn't it? Even if it doesn't, only a serious mental or emotional problem in the son could bring such an outcome, and if despite the parents' best efforts the son did show alarming tendencies, at that point the parents would be obliged to take radical action. Instead of being wise, though, they decide to kill the infant.

Determined to murder, the king and queen make the same mistake that Hamlet's uncle and other murderous literary sovereigns make—they choose to keep their own hands clean (never mind their souls). They give the child to a shepherd, who is to abandon him far away in the wilderness. Human compassion being what it is, the shepherd happily gives the baby to a stranger bound for Corinth. What the king and queen of Thebes don't know can't hurt them—for a while.

The baby is readily adopted by the king and queen of Corinth, who cannot have children of their own. They keep his adoption secret from him, as do the citizens of Corinth except for one drunken man who blabs the truth at a celebration. The young prince, now named Oedipus, ignores the drunk.

When he reaches the age to do so, Oedipus travels to the oracle to learn about his future. He hears the same grim words that his birth mother heard. Horrified, he believes he has no choice but to banish himself from Corinth and never return until both of his parents have died. But he *does* have another choice. He can go to his parents and tell them about the prophesy. They will tell him that he is adopted and that his parents are in Thebes. Considering that he once heard he was adopted, even if it was from a drunk, shouldn't he talk with his parents? Students seek the truth. Victims murder their fathers and marry their mothers.

First, let's knock off the old man. A self-banished prince, Oedipus wanders ancient Greece until he meets an older man so important that he's accompanied by bodyguards. Royal pride swells in the egos of both travelers, so neither offers to step aside for the other. It appears to both that the only logical act is to fight to the death, and thus we have literature's earliest depiction of road rage. Oedipus kills his father and all but one bodyguard, who runs home to Thebes and, embarrassed to admit that he fled from one man, blames the carnage on a group of bandits. The Thebans pour a great deal of time and effort into hunting a fictitious band of robbers and killers. Poor, self-victimizing Oedipus. Most of us think we know who our fathers are, but let's face it—some of us are wrong. Wouldn't it be wise of Oedipus to make a point of never killing men old enough to be his father?

To make matters worse, he seeks out marriage with a woman old enough to be his mother. When a supernatural critter called the sphinx plagues Thebes, the widowed queen sends out word that she will marry any man who destroys the creature and will make that man king of Thebes. Oedipus does so, and he and his, uh, mature bride bring four children into the world. Given the old prophesy, the queen should know better than to marry a man young enough to be her own son, just as Oedipus should know better than to marry a woman old enough to be his mother. Of course, the truth eventually comes out, and in horror, humiliation and shame, the queen commits suicide and Oedipus blinds himself. In time, the children don't fare well either. All of this because every chance the involved parties have to use the prophesy well and make a wise decision, they act like the hasty know-it-alls they are instead of the thoughtful leaders they should be. The oracle's prophesy comes true because no conditions change.

In words I've heard so many times from Ramoth: "What have we learned?"

Four

A Major Revelation

At the same time that Ramoth recommended I read Revelation, he recommended a book called *The Aquarian Gospel of Jesus the Christ*, by Levi H. Dowling. Published in 1908, the work purportedly is derived from the Akashic Records, an otherworldly catalog of every event that has ever occurred. Belief in the Akashic Records has endured for ages among mystics, and Dowling is not alone in claiming to have accessed them. I have not, and while it stands to reason that a record of all things should exist, I can't promise that it does exist. Theologians and others, unsurprisingly, have blasted *The Aquarian Gospel*, just as many reading my words will declare me a mouthpiece of Satan. I've looked briefly into Dowling's life and recommend that others do so as well. He seems honorable to me, especially due to my own experiences, which have assured me that some of us, for whatever reason, really do get to interact with the enlightened side of the spiritual realm.

The four gospels offer a teasingly meager sketch of Jesus of Nazareth. *The Aquarian Gospel* paints Him in full color. It begins with the birth of Mary and follows the childhoods of both John the Baptist and Jesus, then chronicles the entire life of Jesus. While the four gospels tell us nothing about Jesus between the ages of twelve and thirty, *The Aquarian Gospel* follows Him through those lost years, showing Him as a traveler and student visiting and studying with the most learned teachers of India, Tibet, Persia, Assyria, Egypt and Greece. It delves deeper into the three years prior to his crucifixion and reports Him speaking of karma and reincarnation, at least privately to the Apostles. The book hints at a scientifically plausible method Jesus used to become buoyant atop water and even to disappear from sight, and it concludes with the Resurrection, Jesus's later appearances among His disciples and creation of the early "Christine" church.

Personally, I put a great deal of faith in *The Aquarian Gospel,* but as with all written works—or spoken—all readers must decide how it resonates within themselves. I am only one of Ramoth's students—possibly the most devoted one and apparently the only one given to write a book about him—but Yvonne, the channel, is closer to him than I and knows him better than I. Her opinion of the book, influenced by Ramoth himself, is that it is very accurate but not a hundred percent accurate. On this planet, nothing is perfect.

In a college literature class, I learned of a painting by Benjamin Haydon titled "Christ's Entry into Jerusalem." It shows a white-haloed Jesus riding a donkey through a reverent crowd. Oddly, to Jesus's left stands the English poet William Wordsworth and, just beyond him, John Keats. It is known that Haydon, Wordsworth and Keats were all acquainted, but beyond that I wondered why the artist put the two poets in the painting.

"You were both there," Ramoth said.

William Wordsworth, I learned, had been among his many lives the Roman poet Pintar and would be the American poet Allen Ginsberg. In Jesus's time, like myself, he was someone in Jerusalem, and his soul and mine watched Jesus enter the city for the last time and soon afterward would be close at hand to a soul-wrenching event. Knowing that is humbling to me.

Little by little I learned some facts about my life at that time. My name was Simon. I was related to Lazarus, whom Jesus brought back from death, and also to Jesus Himself or possibly Joseph. I became a victim of leprosy, and Jesus healed me, according to Ramoth, restoring fingers that had fallen off. (Indeed, I was the man referred to in Matthew 26 as "Simon the leper.") Yvonne was present too, a part of Jesus's circle.

Also there were at least three other clients of Yvonne. In our present lives, Yvonne, those three clients and I became very close friends. Even the Woman was alive in Jerusalem, a child aware of and saddened by the great injustice.

According to Ramoth, in His youth Jesus had to learn who He was. The knowledge came gradually. An important part of His work on earth was to experience first-hand what it is to be human. Centuries of church doctrine and generations of preachers have shaped our image of Him, an image that needs reshaping. As Raymoth once said, crumbs from His most recent meal were likely clinging to His beard; His feet were often scraped raw, just like those of the people He walked among. Yes, He could walk on water, but He could also trip over a rock. He genuinely loved Mary Magdalene (who was never a prostitute but whom He had cured of mental illness) and likely would have married her had He not known that His time was short and too valuable. Raymoth once mused that the world would be enriched if the descendants of Jesus and Mary Magdalene lived among us.

Typically, Christians say that Jesus came to die for our sins. The idea is simplistic and cannot be more than partially correct. Jesus died on the last day of His earthly life. Was the purpose of every other day of His life simply to make Him valuable on that last day? Raymoth said that He did not come here to die but to live. The universe is a complicated little gizmo with astrological ages that are linked with our progress as a spiritual species, for lack of better words. The dawning of each new age corresponds with the arrival of an avatar who strives to lead us forward. The avatar is a leader, a teacher, a role model. By definition an avatar is a deity manifested on earth. A son of God walking in a human body, therefore, is an avatar—a human being who displays traits of God, such as performing miracles, forgiving sins, etc. He is at least as much a teacher and a role model as a savior. Indeed, are not teachers and role models saviors?

Jesus died for our sins: does the statement not smear each of us with guilt? I've even heard people say that *we* killed Jesus. Scripture illustrates that Jesus's crucifixion was engineered by a mere handful of people, all of whom felt their positions and income threatened by His teachings. Ramoth has said that Jesus never intended for His followers to feel guilty. Whether in groups or individually, He met people where they were and as they were with the purpose of bringing them forward, not cutting them down. The only group He railed against were the rabbis who turned the temple into a mini-mall for their own profit.

We will live, die and reincarnate in this school called earth until we learn all of earthly life's curriculum; then we likely will do it again in some school of *higher* education. The point of our learning is perfection of the soul, and Jesus came to walk our path in order to show us the way it should be walked so that we can be more like Him, so that our souls will evolve in this life. Then, in the next incarnation, we can *begin* farther along life's path, with the opportunity to evolve even further, becoming more and more like our leader, who is also walking life's path. Life is eternal. We can't get out of it. We need to make the best of it. Jesus has walked on earth. He has laid a path for us, a path that leads to the light. We can stay on the path by always turning in the direction of the most light. That's the direction Jesus took. He really is the way.

I once asked Ramoth: "What is heaven?"

His first words of reply surprised me: "Heaven is tunnel."

Tunnel? One aspect of a tunnel is that once we commit to it, we can't veer away from it. We can move quickly or slowly—we can even sit and do nothing for a while—but eventually we have to get up and move on. We also speak of a tunnel as having a light at the end of it. Light symbolizes God. Just as a tunnel is a passageway to light, heaven is the passageway to God. Notice that one steps out of light into a tunnel to travel its length to light, just as we once left God only to work our way back to God. What a wonderfully rich statement Ramoth made in three words—*heaven is tunnel.* It shows that in God's universe we are always accomplishing something, always achieving. I am so relieved that I won't have to spend eternity playing a harp and listening to you play one.

We are washed in the blood of the Lamb. Our sins are cleansed by Christ's blood. Why must Christianity involve so much bloodletting? And why do some Christians utter such gory rhetoric? The idea that sins might be washed away through baptism is a much more wholesome concept, and one that Jesus Himself partook of. A problem with Christianity as it's presented to us in church is that it does not really encourage thought. I once heard a young woman state that because she was a Christian, she didn't believe in dinosaurs and thought that the theory of evolution was nonsense. "You have to have faith," she said. As she used it, the word "faith" meant "absence of thought." I have no doubt that her clergyman would have smiled proudly to hear her. I don't think he would smile at this paragraph, though. In his world, to do too much thinking makes one a heretic. However, I'm sure God has a special place in His heart for heretics: they actually think about Him; they actually look for Him. What did Jesus say—"Seek and ye shall find"?

Having stayed out of churches for most of my life but having thought about God nearly every day of it, I've developed a dispassionate (some might say jaundiced) view of religion. I realize that some people aren't born with a great tendency toward spirituality. For such people religion is essential. It's their way of connecting with God. Even so, the gulf between God and religion is enormous. God *is.* I am absolutely certain of that. God is everywhere and in everything except that which comes from the deepest crevices of evil. God is all things positive. God is love and is eternal. He created us. We did not create Him. But we human beings created religion. We created all of the world's religions. But it is hard to find a religious person—at least in the Western world—who can accept the truth of another person's religion. Virtually every religious person believes that he was lucky enough to be born into the World's One True Religion, yet he can't explain how he knows that to be true. That's because it isn't.

Ramoth has said that if we took the best from each of the religions on earth, we would pretty much get it right. That also means that we would have to delete much from all of the world's religions. So what do we delete?

Suppose we start with everything that tears people apart instead of bringing them together. If we are indeed all brothers and sisters, does it stand to reason that God wants us to be a dysfunctional family? Surely we should also throw out all aspects of religion that portray the deity as negative, spiteful, petty or vengeful. The idea that God values some of us over others needs to go. Surely that idea is nothing more than a function of human prejudice. Prejudice itself is ignorance in action and nothing more. Moses, Jesus, Mohammed, Buddha and other great spiritual leaders agree on all important points. If we must have a religion, why can't we focus on those points of agreement and discard all else?

Therefore, the key to a God-oriented spiritual life is simple. Choose a great spiritual leader. Your cultural background might suggest someone other than Jesus. You must follow your truth. I grew up in a Protestant Christian church and therefore was familiar with Jesus. Because Ramoth—whose words have proven truthful time and again in my life—told me that Jesus was real and is real, I very naturally made Jesus my leader on life's path. He is my role model.

Whoever your spiritual leader might be, assuming that he is honorable and the real thing, make him your role model. But be careful. Someone who comes in the name of a great leader such as Jesus or Mohammed is no avatar himself—he is the priest of an avatar. He or she is not your true leader. Look beyond any priesthood to your true leader. Next, try your best to emulate that leader by following his spiritual path. Learn all you can about your leader so that in times when you must make a decision, you will know what choice to make. I ask myself *What would Jesus do?* Then I have my answer. Those few great souls, our guides to God, will always move in the direction of God's light. The choice with the greatest light is the greatest choice.

If we follow the path of light that leads to greater light, everything else falls into place. Religious dogma is mere noise compared to the truth of God that we can find within us, just by holding to the path. It is dogma that separates the God-oriented peoples of this world. Consider that, please.

Ramoth insists that Jesus will return soon. There are other great souls who have incarnated repeatedly in order to help people on earth. The prophet Elijah, according to Ramoth, did indeed reincarnate as John the Baptist as well as Buddha, Mohammed and Mahatma Gandhi. Just imagine how many times that soul might have lived on earth. It could be here now.

When Jesus returns, Ramoth says, it will be as a lion, not as a lamb. Before, He needed to be a lamb. He was born into a world where might made right, where powerful leaders sometimes declared themselves gods. He was born into a people living under the thumb of Rome, with little hope of improving their lot. He was born among people taught to expect Him to be a great warrior, one who would bring them salvation on earth through victory with swords and spears. Earth had experienced enough of that sort of savior, enough of the proud and haughty.

So Jesus came as a lamb. A lamb can do little to defend itself, and every predator above a certain size would find a lamb irresistible. But the way to God doesn't lead through conquest and plunder. It leads through clear thought, kindness, compassion, love and respect. Humility. A lamb is, indeed, a humble creature. The proud and haughty had their way with the lamb, but even crucifixion hardly stopped it. The impact of that lamb is felt across the world to this day.

Perhaps it is hard to imagine Jesus as the lion. I have some trouble doing that myself. Ramoth explains that the lion will not come as a predator but as a protector. The lamb showed us how to be gentle. The lion will protect Jesus's gentle people from, shall we say, the hyena (my word, not Ramoth's).

Today's world is one of imbalance. We live out of balance with nature. The disparity between the wealthiest and the poorest is out of balance. Certain corporate leaders are bleeding us dry. And scattered among the various nations' heads of state are the most evil individuals on the face of the earth. Who knows? The lion might need only to bare its teeth and show its claws.

When Jesus returns, Ramoth says, it will be with full recall. He will not need to learn who He is, as He did before. When He returns, He will call Himself Jesus. However, as we all know, we on earth have misused His name and God's as well. We turn them into curse words, and some con artists use them for fraudulent purposes. God and Jesus are aware of this, of course, and displeased. Jesus would prefer being called the Disciple—the student. Out of respect, Yvonne and a number of members of her circle, myself included, usually refer to Him among ourselves as the Disciple.

Earlier in this chapter I mentioned the early "Christine" church. In *The Aquarian Gospel* the original followers of Jesus were called Christines. I like that word. I think of myself as a follower of Jesus, a Christine. I am no longer a member of any Christian church. I don't follow doctrine. Doctrine is man-made. It divides people, often even Christian from Christian. I follow the light of God. It beckons us all. It is universally inclusive.

Five

The Holy Grail

After the Crucifixion, after Jesus appeared to His Apostles and certain friends and spoke His last earthly words to them, the Apostles and other disciples set about spreading His message. The Apostle Phillip traveled to Gaul and from there sent word to Mary Magdalene that he could use her help. Accompanied by Joseph of Arimathea, the man who donated his tomb for Jesus's burial, Mary came to Phillip's aid. However, when they caught up with Phillip, he no longer needed them badly and suggested that they travel on to Britain. It was there, at the site of present-day Glastonbury, that something happened, indirectly resulting in perhaps the British people's all-time greatest legend.

Where charming Glastonbury stands now, Mary and Joseph created a center of Christine learning where converts heard of Jesus and His teachings from those who knew Him well. It took time, but from that spot the word spread throughout Britain.

Mary and Joseph each carried an item from what we now call the Holy Land. Mary carried a wooden or ceramic cup that had held the oil with which she had anointed Jesus shortly before His arrest. With that same cup she had collected some of His blood as He hung upon the cross. No doubt the cup was still stained. One can only imagine what it must have meant to her broken heart. Joseph's item was less meaningful, but it would assume more meaning with time. It was a walking stick cut from a thorn tree.

Mary and Joseph must have done some of their teaching at an artesian well now known as the Chalice Well in Glastonbury. Mary probably performed healings there. To this day the well's water is said to have curative properties. Eventually, Mary died and was buried near the well. To mark her grave, Joseph drove his walking stick into the ground.

Although it had been cut from the tree a long time, the stick grew roots and leaves. It became a tree itself and lived for about a thousand years. When the tree showed signs of dying, someone took a cutting from it. That cutting replaced the dying tree, and to this day the walking stick of Joseph of Arimathea spreads its leaves above the grave of Mary Magdalene in Glastonbury, England.

Someone—surely the most trusted student of Mary and Joseph—was given the cup so dear to Mary's heart. Today we call that cup the Holy Grail. The word "grail" apparently has no meaning and is used only in reference to that one cup. Ramoth surprised me by saying that I actually owned an accurate depiction of the Grail. In a book of paintings from the Uffizi Gallery, a major art museum in Florence, Italy, I found the Grail in a work called *The Lazarus Triptych, by* Nicolas Froment, a French artist from the fifthteenth century, who had channeled the Grail's image. The actual composition of the cup can't be determined from the image, but if I had to guess, I'd say that it was created by a potter. It's a cup that flares outward from its base, is white with a blue design painted on, as well as a gold rim, and it has a matching lid, the center portion of which rises in a steep cone. I did indeed find the correct image of the Grail, Ramoth said. The paint is now gone, but the Grail remains hidden and will be discovered as part of the Second Coming. I suppose time has rubbed away the bloodstains as well as the paint, but wouldn't it be amazing to retrieve the DNA of Jesus of Nazareth?

So Mary Magdalene and Joseph of Arimathea died, and the first keeper of the Grail cherished the object and passed it on to its second keeper, who passed it to a third. Time marched on with its endless cycle of battle and conquest, murder and profit. Christines in Britain continued to spread their message among Druids and other folks whom we lump together as pagans.

History, especially old history, is a mixture of precise facts and sometimes conflicting claims that must be sorted through. Into its complex fabric are woven threads of dubious origin and here and there, probably, an outright lie. A word is only as true as the mouth that utters it, and some accounts have been written to flatter, or satisfy, monarchs. Occasionally, Ramoth says things that are at odds with generally accepted history. When this happens, I tend to give Ramoth the benefit of the doubt.

In 1999, when Ramoth first mentioned King Arthur, Merlin and Camelot, I was astounded. I had rather hoped Arthur was real, but the story Ramoth unfolded was so much better than the accepted Arthurian legends. And—like the legends—it involves the Holy Grail.

Let's begin with Constantine the Great (272–337), emperor of Rome. Theories persist that Arthur was somehow descended from him. Ramoth agrees. Constantine himself spent time in Britain and possibly left behind a child from whose line Arthur sprang, or it could have been Constantine's son Constans (322–350), in Britain in early 343, who did the deed. At any rate, a descendant of Constantine was Uther Pendragon, father of Arthur.

Arthur was born very near the Chalice Well, close by Glastonbury's most prominent geographical feature, a tall, conical hill known as Glastonbury Tor. On the other side of that hill, some years before Arthur's birth, Merlin was born. The two grew up in a society well versed in both Christine beliefs and Druidism. Arthur would eventually choose the Christine life, Merlin the Druid life—and a bad version of it at that. Forget the idea that Merlin was a wonderful old wizard. Sorry.

Druidism in itself is not a bad religion. Ramoth speaks highly of the ancient Druids when they were at their best, believing that they were enlightened, spiritual people. I mention them as a phenomenon of the past, but there are practicing Druids today.

I'm sure that the great majority of them are fine people. Merlin eventually got into the practice of human sacrifice, however. God frowns on that, to say the least.

At first, though, Merlin was something of a mentor to the young Arthur, teaching him the best of the Druid ways. But Arthur had another set of teachers too, devout Christines. Probably sensing the negativity inherent in Merlin himself, Arthur chose the Christine path.

Very early in life, Arthur became king of a small part of Britain then known as Camelot. Legend tells us that he was a fierce warrior. Ramoth paints him as a good negotiator as well. Arthur identified as a Celt. Anglo-Saxons, who were beginning to establish themselves in Britain, were hardly being greeted with open arms. However, Arthur created a complex alliance with an Anglo-Saxon king.

We know this king as Percival. The arrangement was that Arthur and Percival would essentially merge their kingdoms, with Percival becoming, at least somewhat, Arthur's vassal. That was a great deal to ask of Percival, but Arthur conceded a great deal too. Percival had taken Arthur's older sister as his wife, and Arthur conceded that a son born of that marriage would succeed Arthur as king of the merged realms. There would be peace between Arthur and Percival, and together they would stand as a formidable foe for anyone inclined to attack. Arthur's sister, incidentally, already had a son, sired by Merlin. His name was Lancelot.

With Percival, Arthur's sister had three more sons. The eldest was Bors, the middle was Gawain—who grew to be 6'7", according to Ramoth—and the youngest Ramoth identifies as Tuck. Bors and Gawain became knights, joining their father at Arthur's Round Table, and the youngest son became a Christine priest. Perhaps Tuck is the person known in legend as Bishop Baldwin, perhaps not. I know that he died at age 35, maybe too young to have become a bishop.

Peace in Camelot was based on a potentially uneasy alliance with Percival. It faced three other threats as well. First was the fact that Arthur himself had a son who matured to be brave and ambitious—an obvious threat to the agreement with Percival. The son was Mordred, also known as Medraut. Another threat was the edgy relationship between Christines and Druids. The final threat added additional danger to the other threats because it was so insidious. It was Merlin himself. He coveted power. As a man of mystery, manipulation and dark knowledge, he had the ability to strike from all sides at once. And he would.

Shortly after I began learning from Ramoth, he encouraged a friendship among two other men and me. We were all regular clients of Yvonne, and the three of us were well educated, with active minds and spiritual natures. One of the men—John—was a few years older than I, the other—Ken—a few years younger. Ramoth referred to us as brothers, and we became like brothers. When he started talking to me about Camelot, he also started talking to them about it. But around that time something interesting happened to me.

One afternoon, shortly after I had broken off the relationship with the Woman, I was simply walking through the kitchen of the little house I lived alone in. Suddenly, in the space of one step, I knew that I had to rewrite *Sir Gawain and the Green Knight.* This story of Sir Gawain of the Round Table is a book-length poem written in the Middle Ages. I was familiar with it and rather liked it but otherwise felt no connection to it. However, I *had* to rewrite it, so rewrite it I did.

The English language has changed greatly since *Sir Gawain and the Green Knight* was written, so I quickly reread the poem translated into modern English, then began writing. I chose to write in unrhymed iambic pentameter (like Shakespeare, but in today's English, of course). I assumed that I would write a summary, perhaps 300 lines in length. No. I wrote some 1,300 lines (still shorter than the original), doing away with the more magical elements of the story and adding the Holy Grail into the mix.

Being drawn to rewrite the work of a dead poet made me suspicious. In a past life, had I been the original author? Yes, Ramoth said. In the United States *Sir Gawain* is usually considered an anonymous work. Another longish poem, *Pearl,* is believed to be written by the same man, and he is commonly referred to as the Pearl Poet. Both poems are grand works. It was humbling to think that I, in a past life, had written them (and consequently frustrated generations of students forced to read them!). Many British scholars believe the Pearl Poet was a man named Hugh Massey, a name confirmed by Ramoth. If I had written about Gawain, *was* I Gawain? Yes, Raymoth said.

As I learned of my life in Camelot, my two "brothers" learned something too. John had been Bors. Ken had been Tuck. In addition, Yvonne's closest female friend among her clients, Leslie, learned that she had been among us but younger than we. Named Egonna, she was Mordred's daughter. And Yvonne? She had been there too, just as she (and Leslie) had been in Jerusalem. She was a psychic named Marrion, a niece of Arthur but a daughter of Merlin. Merlin had offered her great power, yet she wisely declined. She married Gawain.

In a nutshell, here's the story of Gawain and the green knight. During Arthur's New Year's celebration, an unknown "green knight" crashes the party, offering a game. Gawain accepts. The knight hands Gawain an ax and proposes that Gawain strike him a blow on the neck. In one year, Gawain must offer his own neck to the knight. Evidently quite a literal thinker, Gawain beheads the knight. Green knights must be very different from knights of the usual color, however. Instead of dying, the green knight lifts his head from the floor and says essentially: "See you next year at my place—the green chapel. Come alone."

A year later Gawain searches long and hard for the green chapel and eventually comes, nearly dead from cold, hunger and exhaustion, to a castle, where he is welcomed and nursed to good health. His host, Bertilak, proposes a game. For each of the next three days, Bertilak will go hunting afield while Gawain stays at the castle. Whatever Bertilak kills will be Gawain's, and whatever Gawain acquires at the castle will be Bertilak's. Bertilak kills several deer the first day, a boar the second and a fox the third. Gawain spends the mornings of the three days dodging the sexual advances of Bertilak's wife. Each day the wife convinces Gawain that courtly manners require that they at least kiss, so each evening when Bertilak returns, to his amusement Gawain has to kiss him in exchange for the animals Bertilak has slain. However, on that third morning the wife gives Gawain a green sash that supposedly will save him from the green knight's ax, and on the third evening Gawain withholds the sash from Bertilak.

The next morning Gawain arrives at the green chapel. The green knight prepares to behead him. He brings down the ax, stopping just short of Gawain's nape. Then he does it a second time. The third time he strikes Gawain but only nicks him, drawing a little blood. He has shown more courtesy than Gawain showed him. Revealing himself as Bertilak, he explains that the first two ax swings stopped short because in their recent game Gawain was honorable on the first two days. On the third day, though, he held back the green sash, acting dishonorably, and for that received a minor blow.

Gawain returns to Camelot and is hailed as a hero, but he deems himself a failure for being dishonest. His fellow knights begin wearing green sashes in his honor. He continues to wear his as a symbol of shame.

Gawain suffered a blindness that I believe his soul carried into my present life. Once I was talking about Gawain to a college class when one of my students said: "Why didn't Gawain just tap the green knight on the neck? Then the green knight would have owed him only a tap." Oh! Why had I never thought of that? In that moment scales fell from my eyes, and my soul grew just a little. Wisdom is so simple, sometimes so elusive.

I have read critical analyses that see *Sir Gawain and the Green Knight* as a critique of chivalry itself. Certainly, Gawain's adherence to rules of the court cause complications. First, he agrees to a game of trades before learning its ghastly details and then sticks to his agreement rather than show bad faith. Second, he continues with his bargain even after it becomes obvious that he, a mortal, has entered into a game of decapitation with an immortal. Third, he lies to his host. Every decision he makes except for the last one—the lie—is chivalrous, but stupid. If he represents chivalry, chivalry is flawed.

I accept that logic. However, I think there is another, more cryptic, message in the poem, one that I see only bits and pieces of. Ramoth told me that the Pearl Poet wrote about Gawain from memories that came to him. He didn't know they were memories, only that they were thoughts springing from somewhere. The green knight episode in Gawain's life is at least partly true, Ramoth said. Did Gawain behead someone unnecessarily? Arthur did. When the pope sent an emissary to Camelot, wanting money, Arthur sent the emissary's head back to the pope. One would think a simple "No, thank you" would do. Did the Pearl Poet know that fact about Arthur? If so, does it have anything to do with the story about Gawain? Frankly, I don't know. But I do know this.

Arthur had plans that reached far beyond Camelot. He wanted to turn his kingdom over to Bors, just as he had promised Percival. After that he planned to lead his army onto the continent. There he would remove the pope and replace him with Tuck. And he would conquer Rome and make Gawain its king, the better to protect the new pope and his reformed church. Then he would be finished. And all because of Mary Magdalene.

By the time of Camelot, the Christian Church had become quite an organization, almost like a kingdom superimposed over the other kingdoms within its geographic realm. It had its organizational agenda and its religious dogma. It had determined which writings to adopt and which to reject. It did the spiritual thinking for a sizable portion of the world. And it had decided which of Jesus's words His children should hear and which they shouldn't. I refer specifically to the concepts of reincarnation and karma, which Jesus did speak of but which Church officials believed would make people less moral, less afraid of hell. In Britain, generations earlier, though, Mary Magdalene had taught of reincarnation and karma, and that part of Jesus's message was alive and well at Arthur's time. *If Jesus didn't want us to know it, He wouldn't have said it,* Arthur thought, *and if He did say it, how dare the Church keep it from us?*

Arthur envisioned a purer, simpler faith, a Christine faith, his faith, passed unadulterated through his ancestors to him from the guileless, holy lips of Mary Magdalene, who had known Jesus as well as any mortal knew Him.

Arthur's ambition died with him. Ultimately, Camelot fell in a day. Obviously, though, a few complexities led up to that day. The most insidious had to do with Merlin. It is a harmless thing, maybe even a positive thing, to be a practicing Druid, to appeal to the power of earth and spirit to bring good weather, good crops, good hunting, good fortune. But Merlin was a Druid only for show. He was a sorcerer, a practitioner of black magic, a soul made filthy by his greed for power.

Ramoth has verified that on one occasion, Bors, Gawain and other knights accompanied by Tuck interrupted a nighttime ceremony led by Merlin at Stonehenge. A woman was about to be sacrificed when the knights intervened. Merlin's followers fought as Merlin slipped away into the dark and Tuck, driving a cart, ferried the terrified woman to safety. People died in the fight, fighting for the fleeing Merlin.

Merlin was an undermining force, even within Arthur's walls. His influence snaked its way even into Arthur's bed. Far from being the perfect wife and queen, Guinevere was a Druid teenager when Arthur married her to settle a debt with her father. She was not the love of Arthur's life; that woman had died. Guinevere was surreptitiously devoted to Merlin, and she worked to gain control of the Round Table by drugging and seducing knight after knight as well as others among Arthur's staff. Gawain himself was one of her victims, which caused him terrible guilt. Lancelot, Bors and many others fell to her. She had dirt on these men and used it to manipulate them. She was Merlin's spy within the fortress. Through her, he sought to locate the Grail and possess it.

Also, there was Morganna—actually the Morgannas. Merlin had sired a pair of identical twins, whom he kept secretly sequestered. As they grew to adulthood and afterward, he sent them out, never together, under the name Morganna. Thus, Morganna seemed to be full of magic, for she could appear in two places at the same time.

Merlin was behind Druid uprisings against Christines and Christians alike, and he did his best to alienate Arthur's knights from their king. Lancelot, Tristan and Tor fell under his influence. Others might have. Certainly he influenced Mordred, who already believed he should be heir to the throne. Under Merlin's direct influence or not, Percival rebelled.

Mordred took over the fortress and declared himself king, he and Lancelot killing the knights Bedevere and Kay in the process. In a battle outside the fortress walls, Arthur and his loyal knights faced Mordred and his rebels. Arthur was wounded by an arrow through his leg. Gawain and Tristan fought, falling from their horses, and Gawain slew Tristan. Immediately, Mordred, on horseback, attacked Gawain. Gawain dodged the blow as Mordred sped past, then injured the hind leg of Mordred's horse, causing Mordred to tumble. There, face to face with the huge Gawain, whose longer reach and oversized sword gave him an advantage, Mordred retreated.

The fall happened quickly, perhaps that same day. Wounded but able to move, Arthur was praying in his chapel when Mordred crept behind him and ran him through with a sword. Guinevere leapt onto the back of Tuck and stabbed him repeatedly. Bors was also attacked from behind and killed with a sword. Marrion was chased down and killed by a knight dressed in black. Gawain was knocked senseless by a blow to the head and finished with a knife. All were beheaded; Merlin wanted the heads for some of his magic stuff. Interestingly, Arthur's eagle attacked Mordred and blinded one eye.

Camelot was done. But Lancelot, shaken from whatever spell had bound him, did what he could to bring about a measure of justice. He killed Mordred, then Guinevere. He killed Morganna, then finding a second Morganna, killed her too. He killed Tor. Then he killed Merlin. He killed them all without chivalry; he killed them the way they had killed. Eventually, he would kill himself.

Egonna, Mordred's daughter, survived the bloodbath. So did Galahad, Lancelot's son who was still a child. Galahad fled with Arthur's sword and eventually hid it where, Ramoth said, over the centuries it returned to the earth. Galahad is now a member of my circle, but I must respect his privacy and not identify him. However, it's worth noting that he had a later life in England in which he was Thomas Wyatt the Younger, who led the Catholic Rebellion against England's reformation. I was his father in that life, Thomas Wyatt the Elder, a poet, musician and diplomat for Henry VIII; Yvonne was his mother.

On the day Camelot fell, Arthur was 65. Lancelot was 46, Bors 42, Gawain 38, Tuck 35 and Marrion 29. Guinevere was only 19. Just something for numerologists to consider.

Ramoth told us that when she was killed, Marrion was pregnant with Gawain's child. He also told us that in the lives of Marrion and Gawain, Yvonne and I came the closest we have ever been to achieving our higher selves. I don't know what that means exactly, but I do know that we all have something called a higher self which we can tap into ("Shakespeare channeled from his higher self," Ramoth told me), something greater than our own conscious selves—something within us, outside us, maybe both.

The story of Camelot is over except for one detail. Before the battle, before Mordred took over the fortress, Arthur entrusted Gawain with a sacred duty. Monks from the Chalice Well had brought Arthur something that had to be kept safe from Merlin and his marauding Druids. Gawain and Tuck traveled out of danger with the object, following their hearts to the proper spot. There they hid it, there it remains today, and there it will stay until God chooses to place it once again in the hands of men and women. It is the Holy Grail.

Six

A Past-Life Pilgrimage

In early 2000 Yvonne moved to Roanoke, and shortly after that, the two of us decided to go out on a date. We both had the first-date jitters. I remember looking at her as we rode an elevator. She had on a black waist-length jacket, black jeans—and shiny black shoes. I would soon learn that, like me, she was no lover of cities.

By summer 2000 we were a couple. My feelings for her were different from anything I'd known before. She was so honest, so honorable. I could love her without pain or frustration, without doubt. She became the love of my life, and I was privileged to be with her. In a purely spiritual sense, she's a holy person, far greater than I or anyone else I've known.

Encouraged by Ramoth, Yvonne and I, along with Leslie, John and Ken, set out for England. It was to be a spiritual pilgrimage, and we would find the location of Camelot. We would see Arthur and Merlin as well as the old half-brother of John, Ken and me—Lancelot. We planned to stay in Salisbury and travel outward from there simply because Yvonne's mother was from that city. Prior to the trip, in a dream I saw Ramoth standing next to an easel bearing a large map of Britain. Using a wooden pointer, he indicated Stonehenge, Bath and Castle Coombe, a village often considered the most beautiful in England. We all agreed; now we had an itinerary.

The travel agent booked us a bed-and-breakfast. Its address didn't mention Salisbury, but we all assumed that the address represented a specific area of greater Salisbury. Not so. The address took us, in our rented Vauxhall, to a wonderfully picturesque village at least thirty miles west of Salisbury. The bed-and-breakfast was a charming farmhouse, part of which dated to the thirteenth century. Our hostess was a feisty old widow with a need to punish the guilty.

I believe John was first to incur her wrath. He took a walk one morning and returned late for breakfast. Although the rest of us had perfectly fried eggs, both of John's eggs had broken yolks. Then Leslie paid the price for her husband's misdeed. Forgetting about the time difference, he called the farmhouse in the middle of the night, waking the hostess. The next morning Leslie's eggs, and hers alone, smelled suspiciously rotten. She hid them in a napkin and spirited them out to the car. Later, I threw them into a dumpster. On the night before our flight back to America, the lady said: "Since you're leaving in the morning, I reckon you'll not be needing breakfast." Ken put on a thoughtful expression. "No, I think we will need it." From the first day Ken had asked that his eggs be fried without yolks. Oh, but on that last morning the hostess set his plate before him, saying: "I thought you needed yolks for your trip." Yvonne and I made a point of stopping by the kitchen after breakfast each day to compliment the meal. We avoided punishment.

Every morning after breakfast (punitive or not) we walked down the street to a little store that also served as the village's post office. It was a convenient place to pick up the film and snacks we'd need during our travels each day. We always bantered with the couple who ran the store. When we returned home, Yvonne and I visited her mother to tell her about our trip. To our great surprise, Yvonne's mother informed us that after her own mother died, her father moved from Salisbury to the very village where we had stayed and ran the store we had visited daily. Coincidence? No, just a little help from the other side.

Speaking of which, one day we visited Bath, a gorgeous city dating to ancient times, its buildings all of a uniform tan color. We walked about for a while, then decided to visit Bath Abbey. Not knowing where to find it, we asked two men—workmen of some type, by appearance—who sat in a parked white lorry.

One of the men was eating an apple. They told us to proceed to a certain intersection and turn right.

"They were angels," Yvonne said as we walked away.

"What? How do you know?"

"I just know."

Angels or not, they gave us faulty directions—to turn right. Bath Abbey was to the left. At another point in our travels, we asked a person for directions and experienced the same phenomenon. Another angel, Yvonne said.

To this day none of us five doubt that our England trip was guided, that nothing about it was happenstance, that everything about it was meaningful. The fact that we asked for directions twice and that both times our helpers confused left and right—added to the fact that there were two men in the lorry and that the one man didn't correct the other—makes the idea that these people were angels more plausible to me than the idea that of all the people in England, we asked directions exclusively from those who didn't know left from right. Is it possible, then, that when angels manifest among us, they see a mirror image of the world we see? Recently I asked Ramoth about this. He confirmed that the people we talked with really were angels and that when angels materialize among us, what they see is like a reflection. I'd like to know why.

Back to Bath Abbey, tall and impressive. Inside it, for what it's worth, I had a strong sense of déjà vu. I also spontaneously thought that Richard II had stopped there on a journey to Wales. John, who I believe is more psychic than I, had a disturbing experience. Not only did he too believe he had been there before, but he had a wrenching image of a woman he once had loved throwing herself from the abbey's tower.

We traveled everywhere by car, usually with Ken driving and the rest of us waxing poetic about the beauty of the countryside. We also kept an eye out for crop circles, but in that we were disappointed. Next stop, Castle Coombe.

Castle Coombe was once voted the most beautiful village in England. Basically, the village clings to one road that parallels a bold stream so clear that we could see trout swimming in it. Despite the name, there was no sign of a castle. Beyond the stream rose a fairly significant hill.

The day we visited was chilly, with something between mist and rain settling upon us. Tourists wandered quietly. I noticed a man by himself, wearing a MacIntosh coat and a hat, who happened past us several times. He was probably in his late sixties, with white hair and a long, white beard. His trousers looked brand new; the bottoms of the legs were turned up, like cuffs, revealing a red flannel lining. He was near us as we entered the village church. When we came out, he was still nearby.

We loitered in the churchyard for a while. Ken and John discovered a flat rock set into the ground, bearing a plaque that read: "Deep well beneath this rock."

"You don't see that every day," one of them said.

Yvonne and I wandered behind the church.

"Oh, no," she said. "I warned you not to go here."

"What? When? Who were we?"

"You were Gawain. This is the green chapel—this is where it stood."

When Yvonne gets an impression like that, I don't question it. Gawain knelt beneath the ax—and it must really have happened—in present-day Castle Coombe.

We rejoined our group and ambled down the street. The man with the red-lined trousers sat alone on a bench overlooking the stream. Yvonne approached him and spoke.

He could certainly talk. Where were we from? He lived alone and had always lived nearby. He had seen such rains that the stream before him had nearly flooded the village.

Yvonne whispered to me: "Merlin."

Someone asked him about the village's name. Where was the castle?

No one knew if there had ever been a castle, the man said. If there was, it might have been atop the nearby hill. A researcher from Italy had hunted there for signs of a castle but found no proof. Before we parted ways, I realized that all of the man's clothes looked new, as if he had just put them on for the first time. Also, as I looked again at the red at his ankles, I remembered something I had read about Yeats: he believed that red was the color of magic.

"How did you like meeting Merlin?" Yvonne asked the group as we walked away.

Later, when I had a chance to talk with Ramoth about the man, he was adamant that we had talked with Merlin. Except for the modern clothes, I learned, he looked exactly like Merlin. If I returned to Castle Coombe, I would not find him. He hadn't followed us into the church because he *couldn't*. He didn't *wake* the morning after we saw him. For whatever reason, Ramoth gave puzzling answers. My theory is that we saw a manifestation of Merlin, not a reincarnation—a ghost, maybe, but one who could talk and think, like the man who spoke to me when I was a child on a tricycle. Whatever the old codger was, he was real enough that we all saw him and heard him.

We ran into Lancelot in Glastonbury. As we walked the town on foot, he came toward us, carrying a red umbrella. I believe now that the red umbrella was a sign of shame, meant to link him to Merlin. He was six feet tall and thin, a bit over thirty, with red hair that fell nearly to his shoulders. We asked if he knew of a church with a graveyard anywhere in the town. He thought for a moment, then apologized. He didn't know of one. We walked on but soon realized who he was. Ramoth said the man soon realized who we were too. He had been told to look for us just as we had been told to look for him.

Ramoth explained that while this man did look like Lancelot, the Lancelot soul had not been in him until recently. He was what's called a walk-in—something we'll discuss later. Despite appearances, the body was quite ill and likely would not live more than two weeks.

In a reading prior to the trip to England, I asked Ramoth to revisit something he had told me in my first reading—that he saw me as a 38-year-old priest in a churchyard, sad because I had no children. Was that man the Pearl Poet? Yes, Ramoth said. The Pearl Poet, a priest, sired a daughter. He and his lover confessed that to his congregation, some of whom found their act unforgivable. Father Massey, the priest and sinner, had probably already written *Sir Gawain and the Green Knight*. He would soon write another great poem—*Pearl*, about a lost daughter—for someone in his flock fed the little girl poisoned sweets. Compassionately, the priest's bishop gave him a seedling yew to plant in the child's memory. The girl's mother would be poisoned next, then the priest himself. When I got to England, Ramoth told me I should look for the church. I would see a small graveyard and an ancient yew. We were in search of that church and graveyard when we spoke to Lancelot.

About the time of the above-mentioned reading, I experienced a past-life regression under hypnosis. Taken back to the life of the Pearl Poet, I saw myself as a small man in a little boat—with Yvonne—on a narrow stream. I understood then that she was the child's mother. I'm glad of that—except for the murders, of course. Another image I saw was myself lying on a narrow wooden bench, and I knew that the bench was where I always slept. (Ramoth later told me that I had a perfectly good bed but was intent on punishing myself.) I also saw myself at a tiny table beneath an open window lunching on bread, cheese and milk. The last image had me lying again on the wooden bench, this time writhing in pain, especially in my extremities, well aware that I was poisoned and dying and thinking I deserved it. When I came out of hypnosis, I knew one other thing: the Pearl Poet confessed to sheep.

While in England we visited the remains of a castle at Old Sarum, near Salisbury. More about that later. While we were on that site, we saw a picturesque church far below us. We all wanted to visit it, so we made it our next stop.

When we got to the church, the first thing I saw was the great yew tree. As we faced the church, the tree was a bit to its right. To the left were graves. As we walked the grounds, Yvonne showed me where she and the child had been buried. Spitefully, I was buried a good distance away. Nothing marked the graves. I spent a while alone, just looking at the ground where my sweetheart and our child had returned to earth.

Moments later I touched the yew. To think that centuries ago I placed its roots in the soil was more poignant to me than to think that I had written *Sir Gawain* and *Pearl.* Around the church property was a fence. Across the fence grazed a flock of sheep. After centuries, a flock of sheep.

Confession

I confess the belief
that the Pearl Poet
was a tortured priest
with a cherished daughter
born out of wedlock,
that the Pearl Poet
and his shamed lover
bore censure and insults
and lost their child
to poisoned jellied fruit
after they both, bent
sick by guilt, confessed
to the poet's flock.

I confess the belief
that the Pearl Poet
and his shattered lover
accepted a bishop's gift
of a seedling yew
in the child's memory
and planted the tree
in a small churchyard
where it lives today
and casts deep shade,
that the Pearl Poet
wrung to such length
his heart that long
before another poisoned gift
stole his broken lady,
he left his bed
forever, on a narrow
bench took his sleep.

That there may be
compassion in the world,
that the human heart
may channel heaven's grace
the ancient yew attests.
That there is much
besides shoveled three graves.
The Pearl Poet confessed
last to the ears
of sheep grazing near
the church he'd wronged
beyond forgiveness by some,
then from the pasture
and his confessors turned,

walked to his room
and wrote his *Pearl.*

Bread, cheese and milk
beneath an open window's
rowdy, sweet spring breeze
became his last meal.
Upon the hard bench
he felt the poison
grip his stomach, burn
his hands and feet,
knowing at last why
the child first, then
the woman had died.
I deserve this death—
much more, he thought.

I confess that I
have walked where now
a great old tree
shades a churchyard, points
toward sheep its shadow,
have felt beyond words
these thoughts I bear,
have wished we all
could confess to such
as one man did,
who hear, grazing without
distress, our burdened sighs,
who let us lance
sores of the heart,
nor make them theirs
nor rise in judgment.

The churchyard was more for Yvonne and me than for our companions, but it was only a side trip after visiting the ruins of the castle at Old Sarum. The castle was for all of us, at least the site of it was. The ruined castle we toured was built in the late eleventh century by William the Conqueror, but it was built on the site of an older fortress, Ramoth had told us. Camelot.

We traversed the site, inside the castle walls and outside them, feeling the past more than seeing the ruins. I felt that I knew the spot where Bedevere had fallen to Lancelot. Yvonne took me to the spot where she and I had lived in a small stone dwelling. Ken recalled where his chapel had stood. Leslie had a profound experience. She sat on the ground, rocking forward and back, fighting her feelings as she relived a distant day when she, a child, witnessed the deaths of the rest of us and the fall of a realm.

Later, as the five of us stood together outside the rear wall of the castle, a man walked past with his dog. He moved not like a tourist but more purposefully, like someone who came there often to exercise himself and his pet. He wore short pants and, despite his strong stride, had a bandage encircling one thigh. We recalled that King Arthur had been wounded in the leg.

"Could that be Arthur?" someone asked.

"Yes," Ramoth whispered to Yvonne.

I regret that we didn't hail the man, but what would we say?

I remember John as being fairly quiet during the visit to Old Sarum. The other four of us had been there once before. He had been there twice. In fact, he had built the castle that now stood a ruin. In the eleventh century, he had been William of Normandy, most frequently known today as William the Conqueror.

As you might expect, it's kind of an involved story, and as you might already have guessed, it has a connection to Camelot. In 1999 or 2000, while I lived alone in the small house, I had a dream that I think was more of a vision. I saw a man probably in his thirties with black hair parted in the middle and hanging to his shoulders. He also had a full but short black beard, not very impressive. His facial hair was thin. I saw him only from the chest up, and the only garment that made an impression was a black leather vest. Across the shoulders of the vest were narrow black leather strips threaded so as to attach the back of the vest to the front panels. The vest made an impression on me because I had never seen one constructed like that. (I have since, in movies set in the Middle Ages, and I can't promise that I hadn't seen one before, but if I had, I hadn't noticed it.) Behind the man was a stone wall, and on his head was an inconspicuous little crown. His face was boney, his eyes a sharp blue. He looked toward me as if he could see me and was as puzzled as I was to see him. Without the crown, he would look like a guy with a Harley Davidson.

When I asked Ramoth about the vision, he told me I had seen Edward the Confessor. At that time I could have crammed everything I knew about Edward the Confessor into one sentence. Why did I see him? "You were he." I quickly bought a biography.

Edward the Confessor was an Anglo-Saxon king, not considered a true king of England. Nevertheless, he's entombed at Westminster Cathedral alongside the English monarchs. He is never called Edward I. That title belongs to a more properly "English" king—and we'll get to him eventually. Edward the Confessor is so called because he was a pious man, very forthright in his faith and reportedly capable of performin,g healings. He is the only British monarch ever declared a saint, partly because of his professed faith and the healings and partly because years after his death, his casket was opened only to reveal that his remains hadn't decomposed, which was deemed miraculous.

The Danes ruled England beginning in 1013, causing Edward's father, King Aethelred the Unready (yes, really) and family to flee to Normandy. In 1042 it was safe to return, but

Aethelred promptly died, and Edward assumed the throne. By some accounts, the reign went fairly well until in-law problems arose. Edward married Ethel of Wessex, who many lives later would be Yvonne. Her father was Harold Godwin, a nobleman who some lives earlier had been Merlin. Harold and his son Harold Godwinson had power and wanted more. There is no question that they made the king's life harder.

Edward and Ethel had no children. Some historians think Edward was gay. Some speculate that he was too pious to have sex. Others suggest that his problems with Ethel's family convinced him not to produce an heir with Godwin blood. I'm not a historian, only a distant incarnation, but I have a hunch that the hated in-laws theory is valid and in addition that he didn't want a child of his own to have to live the hassle of kingship.

That Edward reportedly brought about healings doesn't bother me. I like a good miracle and have seen a few myself. Did my own motorcycle not defy physics to save me from collision? On another occasion, while working in my garage, I sliced open my thumb. It was a painful, clean cut, deep enough that I could see into it. I looked, wondering when it would fill with blood and overflow. It didn't bleed, though. In fact, the wound started shrinking, closing and getting shorter. Within a minute it was gone, pain and all, and I don't know why. I can surmise, though, that someone on the other side—Ramoth, maybe—was trying to make a point that I still haven't grasped, but I'm grateful for it.

I have a theory that Edward's ability to heal is related to the fact that his corpse didn't decompose normally. If a person has within his body an unusual energy that can heal others—or even if he just channels it through his body—does it not stand to reason that that same energy might heal his own body, maybe even help it withstand the effects of repeated doses of poison? In an obvious moment of weakness, Edward agreed to name Harold Godwinson, his wife's brother, as his successor. But this occurred well after he had already promised the throne to his distant cousin, William of Normandy. In a previous life Harold Godwinson's father had been Merlin, the schemer and sorcerer. Does the poisoned apple ever fall far from the poisoned tree? My conjecture is that Harold had been perhaps drugging and certainly poisoning Edward for quite a while. Finally Edward died, his body already essentially embalmed.

Harold happily made himself king and reigned just long enough for an enraged William of Normandy to bring his army across the Channel and do him in at the Battle of Hastings. I assume that Harold's body rotted quite normally.

And what about William, thereafter known as William the Conqueror? As mentioned earlier, many lives before, he had been Sir Bors of the Round Table. Interestingly, as William he built St. Michael's Tower, which still stands atop Glastonbury Tor, near the birthplaces of both Arthur and Merlin, overlooking the Chalice Well. And, of course, he built his castle on the footprint of Camelot. Just a coincidence, right?

In the early 2000s, I asked Yvonne to regress me to the life of Edward the Confessor. I found myself in a large dining hall with a long table where nearly twenty people were seated. Edward, looking older than when I had seen him in a vision, sat at the head of the table, eating a duck's leg, which he held in his hands. I spontaneously knew a great deal about what was happening. We were at the home of someone who seemed to be named Rathchild—or something like that. Edward liked this nobleman because of their mutual interest in hunting. Generally, he disliked visiting nobles. He looked at me and chuckled: "They think I'm special. They make me sit at the head of the table and feed me legs because they're easy to hold." I returned from the regression believing that Edward was a humble man who didn't especially like being king and saw some humor in the way his subjects exalted him. I think I could be friends with such a man.

Afterward, I wrote the following monologue in which Edward speaks from his deathbed. The form is loosely based on that of Anglo-Saxon poets, with lines featuring a caesura (pause) between the first two stressed syllables and the last two stressed syllables of each line and a consonant (sometimes vowel) sound in the first half of each line repeated in the second half. Read it—there will be a quiz Monday.

Edward the Confessor

I cast from my mind the men who attend me
and, taken by thought, travel alone,
a man on a horse—a humble priest
or a pious knight a part way come,
some yet to go, in God's company.
On such a ride one rainy spring
I met a man bound for a market
pushing a cart, his feet in the cold,
the slippery ruts and pocks of the road.
From saddle to mud, dismounted I stood,
spoke of the misery springtime makes,
summer's hard work, winter's gall.
What might a king answer a man,
I asked. He told me all is toil,
is shiver or sweat. Would I say to God
on his behalf that life is heavy,
cold and damp? God hears a king.
"I own more stones than you," I said.

Clouds take blue sky, then, tattered, break.
Blue sky holds court; then come the clouds.
From seed to bloom, from bloom to seed.
I cannot say what is a king

but say all men make small tracks
on the same road. Some rue the mud,
some watch the sky, some mark the wind
on face and hand. Some fret; some act.
Once I sat admiring a sword.
As thoughts wandered, my thumb split
on the cold blade. I waited for blood,
waited for pain, watching the flesh
deeply gape. God endeavored
to bind my hand with heaven's will.
No blood poured out nor pain flowed up
from the wide cut, but while I watched,
the wound grew small, and smaller grew,
the skin closed without a scab,
my thumb made whole—heaven's pledge.
My pledge to heaven, a whole hand
in the Maker's service to serve men,
nor did I choose but chosen was.
In my long life I have chosen little.

Secluded, protected, declared precious,
I chose nothing in hushed childhood.
My first burden, being a child.
A lone pleasure, learned young,
only hunting lured me happy.
Only the hawk, the horse, the hounds,
these and times alone in my thoughts,
musing on God, then stilling my mind
to hear the voice, see the visions...
Edith knew I loved her enough,
as a common man would have made an heir
to a common life, but not to a king's.
Where are the pleasures attending power?

What day in reign has dull dread
not weighed me weary? I should not wish
life from my own so little joy.

From his dying wife a poor man walked.
Two days he hurried, alone and hungry
in winter's cold to find his king.
"Sire, will you save her? Wasting, she sighs
of God's flock gathering near."
"Let us pray together. God alone,
not I, can heal," I said to him.
Whether she lived I never learned
nor wished to know, for who could want
the burdens that others seek not to bear?

I have heard some call me a weak king.
I have kept the peace, despite the counsel
of those who would war. I have worn the cross
as well as the crown. It worries the heart,
the crown, the head. The heart is heaven's,
the head man's. To herd toward God
a stiff-necked race—for that I ruled,
in that I failed. Too feeble to work,
I listen to Harold, hear him crow.
I wheeze as he frets with what I cannot...

Years make their round in sun and rain,
in wind and cloud. Our lives are clay
heaped on their wheel. From childhood's while,
turning, we pass. At the Maker's pinch,
if our souls will to be God's work,
we rise to duty, as I once rose—
my hair so black, my blue eyes bright,

hollow my cheeks, my jaws and chin
beneath a shallow, wispy beard,
my feet light, and firm my hands.
Oh, did I hold my head high,
and thus the crown. And thus the crown.
From bed the king now cannot rise.
What God erects our days erode.

I ramble and think, think and ramble.
The Maker's pinch. How many men
bear hearts bent to be God's hands?
The deeds of men great damage make.
Detached from God, a long way gone
from heaven's grace, in thoughtless greed
most men forget their past with God,
forget the pearls of heaven's petals,
the silver and gold of heaven's garden,
forget why God has sent them forth…

Oh, how I laughed to myself at life.
At head of so many tables I sat,
lines of faces to left and right,
many too earnest and most seeking favor.
How funny it seemed, sometimes, at a feast
that to honor this sinner all were assembled,
that for this man who would wish no more
than to be God's servant so much fuss,
such vain endeavor, such show of devotion.
What am I fed now? Why does it feel
that what sustains me steals my will?
I liked the hunters. Hounds and hawks
measure us all by the men we are,
not by title, crown or tithe.

By the measure of beasts, then, men know men
though open hands have often hidden
deceit and greed, which smiles conceal.

I see, as often I have seen—
when closing my eyes, I eased my mind—
the stone wall, the wooden gate,
the gray-haired monk who greets me there,
beyond, the blossoms—fragrant blessings
angel-tended—then the temple.
There I shall bend before the throne
of one whose crown was woven thorns.
Yet king is He, and there no king
am I, but kneeling, a pilgrim knight
home from my journey, by heaven's grace.

In heaven's grace I heave and groan.
These days are short, are dark and damp.
So late it seems, and long I have lain
in this cold room, where many contrive
a little comfort while I linger.
Some men have contrived the deaths of kings...
I find much fault in my food and drink.
They tell me sickness sours my taste.
I listen to Harold, hear his words.
I hear many things, yet still I think,
finding such fault in my food and drink,
that worms will never want my flesh.
I listen to Harold, hear him fade.
I free from my mind the men who attend me.
Taken by thought, I travel alone,
a man on a horse—a humble priest
or a pious knight a part way come,
some yet to go, in God's company.

Now let's turn to the other Edward, Edward I of England, also known as Edward Longshanks due to his considerable height. Edward's father, King Henry III, named him after Edward the Confessor, and the boy grew to be a great admirer of King Arthur, which shouldn't be surprising considering that Ramoth identifies Longshanks as the reincarnation of Sir Bedevere. As king, Longshanks meddled a bit too much in the affairs of Scotland and stirred the ire of one William Wallace, a man even taller than he, a man who in a prior life had been Sir Lancelot, who slew Bedevere in Camelot.

William Wallace, now Scotland's national hero, led an insurrectionist war against England. For perhaps a year before our trip to England, Ramoth had referred to "William" as the fourth brother in the group of Ken, John and me. Not only were we all in Camelot together, but we—and other friends—were together in Scotland too. A great ally of Wallace was Andrew de Moray, a fierce comrade who was mortally wounded at the Battle of Sterling Bridge. Today he's Ken. John was Robert the Bruce, whose allegiance wavered a bit but eventually landed on Wallace's side. In time he became the Scottish king and won the war Wallace began. Wallace had a brother, John—I was he—and found an ally in King Stephen of Ireland, whose sister I married. Today she is Yvonne, and Stephen previously was Galahad. And Leslie? She was Elizabeth de Burgh, who married Robert the Bruce, was captured and spent eight years imprisoned by the English.

Shortly after Longshanks died, Wallace was captured and gruesomely executed in London, his severed head displayed on a pike on London Bridge. The things that passed for decorations in those days. In 1309 brother John's head met the same fate.

So many lives, so much bloodshed, so much karma, so much history. Remember where all these British episodes began. A humble woman with a story to tell came from Jerusalem carrying a blue and white cup. To Arthur the story was worth fighting for. To Merlin the cup was worth fighting to possess. Neither man got what he wanted, but the clash between them stirred dust that has yet to settle. The human story is always about good and bad, light and shadow, love and envy. What does it mean?

Seven

More Past Lives

What does it mean, indeed? I hope someday to know. Of course it seems outlandish that so small a group of souls should take up so much history. Of course it seems outlandish that five people, led by a disembodied spirit, should travel to southern England, interact with angels and whatever the men we met in Castle Coombe, Old Sarem and Glastonbury were, experience past-life memories and in some cases contradict history. From the outside it must seem like a colossal hoax. From the inside—to me, at least—it seems like a colossal undefined responsibility.

We five people who traveled together are all normal human beings except for this one aspect. Most of Yvonne's friends are unaware that she's a psychic. Most people who know the rest of us have no idea that we're—well, whatever we are. People I've worked with probably remember me as rather socially dull. Of the thousands of students I taught, some knew that I grew Christmas trees, some knew that I had horses, some knew that I dabbled in poetry—and that's about all they knew.

I've put off writing this for over twenty years. Why would anyone want to dump ridicule on himself? Yet I have known nearly from the beginning that I would write this. Ramoth told me. I think it's part of the "great spiritual purpose" that I heard myself allude to during my second session with him.

No, I don't know what the story means, but let's continue.

Yvonne has always been drawn to the name Oliver. She named first a bird and later a dog Oliver. I wonder if that comes from a deep memory. According to Ramoth, I was once named Oliver—or rather, the French form, Olivier. Yes, I refer to that same Olivier who was second in command to Roland, the hero of the long French poem *Song of Roland*. Roland (Bors), the nephew of Charlemagne (Arthur), is leader of the rear guard as Charlemagne's army returns home from fighting the Moors in Spain. Attacked by a superior force, Roland chooses to fight to the last man despite the fact that by blowing a great horn, he can summon help from the main army. It's clear that Olivier doesn't understand Roland's motive. Finally, just before dying, Roland blows the horn. Charlemagne's army arrives to find their comrades all dead and the Moors gone.

The poem comes tantalizingly close to its completion but remains unfinished. Someone added to it this last line: "Ci falt la geste que Turoldus declinet." Scholars argue about the line's meaning. Ramoth told me that just as I was Olivier in one prior life, I was the poem's author in another. However, I feel no particular attachment to the poem or to the life of Olivier. I must admit, though, that bringing a project almost to completion and then never finishing it does remind me of myself.

Ramoth told me an interesting fact that the poem doesn't mention, and that fact fits into a pattern. He said that in traveling across the Pyrenees from Spain, Charlemagne was actually in possession of the Ark of the Covenant, which he had wrested from the Moors. In that case, if Roland knew what Charlemagne possessed but Olivier didn't, now we can understand why Roland was loath to call back the army—which could put the Ark at risk—and why Olivier couldn't fathom Roland's actions.

The Ark of the Covenant's involvement would explain why an otherwise minor battle became worthy of its own long poem, and it might suggest a reason why the poem is incomplete. Suppose Turoldus did finish the work and chose to discuss the Ark somewhere near the end. I suppose he or someone else could have been tasked with rewriting the ending so as not to bring attention to the Ark's whereabouts, but a far more expedient solution—and certainly more bureaucratic—would be simply to chop off the end of the work and write "Ci falt la geste que Turoldus declinet," whatever that means, exactly.

And what about the Ark itself? According to Ramoth, Charlemagne hid it somewhere in the Pyrenees, but unlike the Holy Grail, either some line of individuals knew its secret location or someone found it, for it has been moved. Like the Grail, it is waiting.

Of course, when we think of the Ark of the Covenant in the Christian era, we think of the Knights Templar. Ramoth talked more extensively to Ken and John than to me about the Knights Templar, but he said that all three of us were members. As with Olivier, I don't feel that connection, but that might simply mean that I have no karma left from a life among the Knights Templar or perhaps that I possess only aspects of that life.

The next to last remaining past life that I know of from Europe during the early Christian era took place in a monastery in present-day Scotland. I believe it was the next life following that of Gawain. There the Mordred soul and I got to work out our issues. As monks and scholars, together we wrote *Beowulf.* The former Mordred wrote most of the poem. I added the final episode, about Beowulf and the dragon. Ramoth said that Cynwulf, most recently the Nobel-Prize winning Irish poet Seamus Heaney, added a few lines. For several decades I hoped to cross paths with Heaney, but he died before that could happen. I have much enjoyed his translation of *Beowulf.*

Now to Elizabethan England by way of my freshman year at the community college. In Chapter 1 I mentioned showing my verse to a professor there, whose name was Clyde Jones. He was the first to read my poems and encourage me. I took several classes under him and occasionally saw him during the next few years. He urged me not to major in English because I would make too little money and not to become a college professor because my job would be taken by a computer. So much for advice. In 1980–81 and from 1985 until his retirement in 1990, I worked alongside him at the college, and after he retired, the two of us remained friends until he died in 2001. He led a lonely life, I believe a sad one, and I felt sorry for him.

According to Ramoth, he had been my father in London in the late 1500s. I was a little boy when my mother died and he, beside himself in grief and poverty, could think of nothing to do but abandon me on the street and hope for the best. At some point I fell into the clutches of someone who planned for me to be an evening's entertainment. I was present in a tavern when a brawl erupted at a table and a young man was fatally stabbed through the eye. That man was the poet and playwright Christopher Marlowe, and in the chaos I escaped into the night. Evidently people were kind to me often enough that I managed not to freeze or starve. One of my benefactors, ironically, was another poet and playwright, one who missed his own children, a considerable distance away. His name was William Shakespeare, and centuries later he would be good to me again. At that point, I was able to be good to him too.

Eight

"Shakespeare Is Watching"

In summer 1998 and spring 1999 I wrote two plays, the only plays I've ever written. Both are full-length two-act works, and both came to me during the time when I was fighting my feelings toward the Woman. I began the first while she was away at the seashore for a week. Originally I was to accompany her there; then she uninvited me. Even so, I believe we spoke by phone every night she was gone. In eleven days I had the play finished except for some minor revisions.

Called *A Rose in a Bottle,* the play is set in early 1939 in southern France, where William Butler Yeats lies dying. Striving for artistic rather than literal truth, I wrote the play as it came to me. I'm certain that a good bit of it was channeled. Knowing that her husband's end is at hand, Mrs. Yeats has called in his current mistress, Edith Shackleton Heald (this part is strange but true) and his friend the poet Ezra Pound. Maud Gonne, who has obsessed him nearly his whole life, also arrives. Visible to the audience but not to the mortals on stage, four of his dead friends arrive as well—the infamous Oscar Wilde, the playwright John Millington Singe, his one-time lover Lady Olivia Shakespear and the actress Florence Farr. The ghosts, being already dead, take death much more lightly than the mortals do and provide a fair measure of comedy while a fairly equal measure of tension brews among the mortals. Both sets of characters relive moments with Yeats as the play works to make sense of his life. At the end Yeats dies, his soul hopping from the deathbed invisible to all mortals, yet he and Maud dance a bit before Yeats cavorts off stage, accompanied by the other ghosts. In death Yeats finds some sort of peace with his beloved and, hopefully, his own tormented heart.

The community college where I taught was fortunate to have acquired the much over-qualified Bart McGullion as an adjunct professor. A playwright, director and actor whose credits included Hollywood and Broadway, Bart became a supporter of mine after we met and I wrote an article about him for the faculty newsletter. In those days the college presented several plays a year, and one day I mentioned to Bart that I had written a play. As soon as Bart saw it, he wanted to produce it.

A funny thing happened, though. In early 1999 I decided one afternoon to go to a movie alone. With a huge diet drink and a tub of popcorn to match, I settled in to watch *Shakespeare in Love,* which was getting good reviews. I ate, I drank, and the movie began. From the get-go, I felt dissatisfied with the film—yet I didn't know why. I ate more, drank more and realized that I definitely wasn't enjoying the film. I would finish the popcorn and the drink, I told myself. They were paid for. Maybe I would walk out on the movie, but the salt, butter and carbonation had to be consumed first. Finally they were—and I just had to leave. That was strange, for I had never before walked out on a movie, yet I had sat through many far worse.

Moments later, as I got into my car, I realized I was shaking. Tears slid down my cheeks, yet I didn't know why. They *weren't* my tears. I personally wasn't upset, but something inside my head was. Words passed through my mind: *It's all wrong. You have to fix it.* Oh—I was pretty sure who was talking to me. *Pick up the pen,* the silent voice said. *I don't know what you want. I'm sure I can't do it,* I thought.

Pick up the pen.

I drove home and picked up the pen. Here's what I wrote, almost without thinking:

O God! O Great Munificent! Sweet God!
How often have I fallen to my knees
in tears at beauty Thou hast channel'd me?

I am undone from quaking heart to eye,
beholding this fair verse, these lovely words
that by Thy grace poured *to* me and thence *through* me.
What have I done to warrant such a smile?
My feet have walked the ways of sin; my hands
have plung'd unto the elbows in desire.
Yet Thou hast dawn'd to shine on me the light
immortal of the word that even in
the harden'd hearts of jaded men dieth not,
and I am humbl'd, on my knees and weeping
to be first to see such language writ.
O God, Thou lift'st me up with scribbl'd love,
and can I not but publish unto men
what Thou hast whisper'd to my wretched ear?
If this brief life should be my paradise
and through eternity I'm damn'd to burn,
so be it, Holy Author. I am paid—
no poet, I, but scriv'ner at Thy will.
O beauty manifest upon the page,
O grace of God made audible to man—
and I was first to see it, first to hear.

Wow. After I scribbled those lines and then read them, there were more tears on my cheeks, only this time they *were* mine. I knew exactly what was happening. I was channeling the greatest poet of them all. I was channeling William Shakespeare.

That afternoon in meditation I learned that in this play Shakespeare would be writing *Richard II*. I had read *Richard II* in college but had only a vague memory of it. My way of enjoying Shakespeare for years had been to open a play and read a page or so for the sheer power and beauty of the language, but before dinner that day I reread *Richard II* from start to finish.

I think it was that very evening that I was at the college. Bart McGullion was directing a rehearsal for William Inge's *Bus*

Stop, and the Woman had a role in it. Outside the auditorium I showed what I had written to Bart, telling him that was all I had done so far.

"Forget the other play," Bart said. "We're doing this one."

When I think back on that scene, I believe it was one of the greatest "normal" moments in my life. No one before or since has ever shown that much faith in me.

I wrote the play in about a month. Sometimes I would be wakened in the middle of the night to get up and write. At work I put off giving essay assignments to make more time for writing. I wrote during my office hours and virtually all day during weekends.

Shakespeare's Latest Play is the title. Rather than the five acts that Shakespeare and his contemporaries used, it fits into two acts but with a total of five scenes. Like my first play it features supernatural beings on stage, visible and audible to the audience but not to the mortal characters. Shakespeare's muse is on hand to help him write *Richard II*. Essentially an angel, she has arranged for the soul of Richard to be dragged up from hell to serve as a sort of technical advisor. Until the last moment Richard clings steadfastly to his pride, which is what landed him in hell in the first place. But as the play progresses and he sees the courtier Edward de Vere and another man conspire to tempt Shakespeare into abandoning plays in favor of narrative poems that the two men can publish and benefit from financially, Richard rises up to save the playwright from selling out by turning away from his true calling. That act potentially saves Shakespeare from a great mistake and releases Richard from damnation. As with my first play, while writing this one, I had no idea where it was headed until I was far enough into the second act that I deduced its inevitable resolution.

The play is written entirely in iambic pentameter, over 1,900 lines of it, and it maintains Elizabethan English throughout. It features six soliloquies, a love interest, a wise fool, a rhymed couplet at the end of each scene and in de Vere and his friend two villains—although they really aren't very villainous, just opportunistic. And a ghost, of course. Richard is somewhat like a classical tragic hero, but in this case he has already suffered the tragedy and is paying for it but redeems himself. In this way *Shakespeare's Latest Play* resembles my earlier play in that a tragedy becomes resolved after death.

Maybe this suggests a new type of literature to go along with tragedy, comedy and all of their syntheses. All it takes is a writer who sees death as a bump in the road instead of the end of the line.

I spoke with Ramoth several times while writing the play. Some of it was dictated word for word by Shakespeare. In other places he provided the content and I the wording. In a few spots where Shakespeare is being praised to high heaven, I had the feeling that I was on my own. Shakespeare is probably the most polysyllabic of poets, unless T.S. Eliot edges him out, yet I don't see this play as being highly polysyllabic—which means using big words. Maybe that's my influence on it. I do know that I couldn't have written the play by myself. I'm not that good. Ramoth said that Shakespeare had waited through the centuries for the poet who could write his latest play. I think he meant that Keats wasn't right for the job and neither was Yeats. All three of us could handle the iambic pentameter, and all three of us owed him a karmic debt for showing kindness to a street urchin, but maybe only I could hear him give dictation. I was given a "little jewel," Ramoth said. I am deeply honored.

In the play the character Shakespeare utters a speech to his lover, Emilia Bassano Lanier, a historical figure who was a lady in Queen Elizabeth's court and a fine poet in her own right. In it he describes the act of channeling, which I believe he was well aware of. Ramoth says the he channeled from his own higher self.

Thou makest merry, which doth lift me up.
But I feel mov'd to give these words to thee,
for I do love thee much, and love to write,
and I would have one love the other know.
Emilia, ere now I told thee once
and fain would quote again how 'tis I write:
A voice not mine own in me doth speak,
a mental eye not mine alone doth show
me scenes drawn richly and in colors bright,
an ear not these thou see'st doth collect
what breath ne'er say'th till I have writ it down.
I can but tell that I am told to write,
that I but write what I am blest to hear,
that I am but a channel from beyond
the veil our senses drape about our souls,
that I have opened wide my heart to man—
perchance was born with heart so strangely formed
(I cannot say when't happened, where or why)—
and that I would but be the mouth of God,
if God it be that useth me to speak,
that I would raise the fallen where they lie,
as any man of conscience fain would do,
that I would ladle pride a sip of bile,
that I would see the English govern'd well—
yea, the men and women of the world—
or better far, would see each man and woman
govern well the self, and clip the claws
of those who rule in strength but wisdom spurn
and greed embrace. Emilia, I am
but what I am, and I am come to thee,
my heart upon my palms, for thou canst see
in me the sketch of what I am, the lines
conflicting, doubl'd, rubb'd to smudge, complete,
aborted and begun anew that, all

as one, consign me form and would imply
some content, some compassion, some intent.

You didn't skip the poetry, did you? If so, go back and read it. It's a bit otherworldly. Also, in the play, Shakespeare actually writes a sonnet. I gave it an apt title.

Shakespeare's Latest Sonnet

A king in tatters, bow'd before disgrace,
Thou see'st in me, yet lov'st me even so,
And sweet thy touch that doth thyself abase
To raise a lofty realm from rubble low.
Thy name upon men's tongues shall scandal be
As my poor name doth hound thee down the street,
And all because thou tarry'd some with me,
Who could but trade my pain for favors sweet.
Yet thou art yellow beams that steer my days,
And eerie beams that lure my dimmer hours.
By thy whisper do I seek new ways,
And from thy strength do I obtain new pow'rs.
Thus wouldst thou raise me to a brilliant height
Though thou must know 'twill dim thee in my sight.

True to his word, Bart McGullion did produce the play. He directed it and played the role of Richard II. His son Jeff, an excellent actor, played Shakespeare. Several local actors and actresses as well as students filled out the cast. The college chose not to seek publicity for the work, however. The week it was running, I read an article in the local newspaper about someone over a hundred miles away who had written a play and was staging it in his apple orchard. The only mention my play got was a small notice in that part of the newspaper that gave the times of various flower club meetings. Nevertheless, participants in the production did a fine job of hanging fliers around the community, and actually a good many people saw the play. Among them were my fourth and sixth grade teachers and a surprising number of mathematics professors. The entire English department stayed away, however. Maybe for some reason my closest colleagues weren't meant to see the play.

During the time I was writing, Shakespeare communicated to me almost as if the two of us were conversing. The connection—the channel—that he created between us allowed me to learn things about him. I got an image of him sitting at his table, measuring his lines as he wrote. All poets who write in iambic pentameter as Shakespeare did have to keep count of the five stressed syllables in each line. As he constructed a line in his head, he typically kept count of the stresses with his left hand, straightening or closing the pinky finger, then the ring finger and so on until he got to the thumb, which marked the end of the line. I don't think that's uncommon—I do it myself—but I did see him alone in a dim room, doing exactly that as he wrote by candlelight.

Another fact I learned has to do with an often-quoted statement about him in an elegy written for him by his fellow playwright Ben Jonson, a comment that Shakespeare "had small Latin and less Greek." Many people have tried to explain why, in a poem praising the man, Jonson made that critical remark. Shakespeare gave me to know that Jonson's words were a joke about Shakespeare's behavior. He went among his friends and colleagues prefacing insightful remarks with: "Well, I know small Latin and less Greek, but"—boom! Something profound.

I gained a sad knowledge about Shakespeare's death. He retired from theater and returned to Stratford-upon-Avon in failing health. He had been prescribed mercury, which we now know is a dangerous poison, and he relied on his daughter Susannah to measure his dosage. He shouldn't have. Imagine—in a poll William Shakespeare was found to be the most admired

English person ever, but to his daughter he was just a nuisance keeping her from a little inheritance.

A year or so after I wrote the second play, Yvonne and I were married. For several years she channeled Shakespeare occasionally. He told me that he had given me the first play as well as the second and that he did it because he was worried about my mental and emotional state due to the obsession with the Woman. One time he remarked about the picture of him that I hung in our house. When I wrote a funny story that involved a Cadillac, he wanted to know what a Cadillac was. He referred to Yvonne as "a most agreeable woman" and made jokes about our English bulldogs. Curs, he called them. He asked why I wrote using a keyboard instead of with ink and paper. Also, he gave me some advice that I now think was about relationships. "It is more important to be a man," he said, "than to be a writer."

Only recently I recalled something that came to me shortly after I began practicing automatic writing in 1997: "Shakespeare is watching." Evidently he was.

Since I was cognizant enough to have an opinion on the matter, I've considered William Shakespeare the king of poets, at least in the English language. Surely he was the greatest playwright to write in verse and the greatest poet to write plays. While I state that Keats and Yeats are my two favorite poets, I readily place them at the foot of the throne of Shakespeare. His name doesn't enter into a discussion of favorites because other poets don't compare to him.

From Ramoth I've gained quite a few facts about the Shakespeare soul. I once incorrectly surmised that Shakespeare had been Lancelot based on the idea that the word "Lancelot" could be derived from "lance zealot," which might describe someone who "shakes" a "spear." Only in my mind, according to Ramoth. Shakespeare had been Quintus of Smyrna, who wrote the long poem *The Fall of Troy*, which picks up the story of the Trojan War where Homer's *The Iliad* leaves off. Quintas was able to create such a seamless sequel to *The Iliad* because in a past life he had written it; he had been Homer. He was also the Roman poet Virgil, who might be best known today as a character in Dante's *Divine Comedy*; he serves as Dante's guide through hell and purgatory in the work's first two books, *The Inferno* and *The Purgatorio*. Then he was Dante himself. (T.S. Eliot wrote: "Dante and Shakespeare divide the modern world between them. There is no third." Maybe there's no second.) Shakespeare has also painted; he was my favorite of the Italian Renaissance painters, Raphael. I've heard it said that none of his contemporaries could match the humanity in Raphael's paintings. What writer has matched the humanity in Shakespeare's plays?

At the time of Jesus, I very likely knew Shakespeare in or around Jerusalem. He wrote one of the four gospels, the Book of Luke. Luke was not one of the Twelve Apostles, but he certainly was a disciple of Jesus. It's accepted historically that Luke painted a portrait of Jesus on a wooden door, the only painting of Jesus made from life. Unfortunately, the door is long gone.

As of 1999, when he was dictating a play to me, Shakespeare wasn't incarnated in an individual body on earth, Ramoth told me. But I had aspects of Shakespeare, he said, as do most true poets.

Nine

The Human Soul

What does it mean to have aspects of another's soul? Perhaps you should know—you have them. So do I. So does everyone. In fact, plenty of people have aspects of our souls.

I have no idea what a soul looks like, how big or small it is, how it travels or anything like that. I know it's there, but it's totally abstract to me. So in order to illustrate how aspects work, let's image that the soul is liquid and that we carry it around in some sort of container—let's say a big bucket.

Friends and family members usually have aspects of one another's souls. It's as if we go around with our buckets of liquid soul and a small dipper, and we ladle some of our soul into their buckets and they ladle some of their souls into ours. We have traded aspects. The trading of aspects allows us to share one another's earthly experiences on a plane higher than earth. Also, the shared aspects strengthen the bonds between us on earth. We can trade aspects back and forth even while alive on earth; it happens on that higher plane, but we're likely to experience some correspondence to the trade here on this plane.

John, Ken, Leslie, Yvonne and I bonded together prior to our trip to England because we all shared aspects. We shared aspects because of what we had experienced in past lives, and those shared aspects created easy paths to friendship among us.

Not only do we have aspects of people in our immediate lives, but we can have aspects of people we don't even know. In some cases we'll eventually meet those people, but in some cases we won't. We also have aspects of people in the past, which is an interesting idea to consider. For example, if I possess an aspect of Shakespeare, I also possess an aspect of everyone Shakespeare was in his own past lives. Thus, I possess aspects of Dante, Virgil, Luke, Quintus of Smyrna, Homer, Raphael, etc. I gain something, if only a little, from each of those aspects. You and I each embody aspects of probably thousands of lives from the past. Just think what a rich pot of soup your own soul must be.

While undergoing a reiki session in or around 2003, I suddenly realized that I had aspects of the American poet Theodore Roethke. When I asked Ramoth about that, he explained that in the 1940s, Roethke received aspects of Yeats (who died in 1939), which helped him as a poet. When Roethke died in 1963, those aspects returned, which means they came to me because, he said, I'm a full reincarnation of Yeats (and Keats).

An important advantage of sharing aspects is that we also share wisdom on the soul level, the kind of wisdom we gain mostly through experiencing karma. Sharing lessons learned helps us all move forward on life's path more efficiently, more quickly. God gives us karma to teach us, not to punish us, and a lesson learned vicariously, if it is truly learned, allows us to speed ahead without having to deal with a karma-inducing roadblock.

People speak of good karma and more often of bad karma, but all karma is a pathway out of the human mess we're in. Karma presents us with good things in life and frustrating things. A student of life considers both to be lessons. By recognizing them as lessons and learning from them, we retire bits of karma. Once we run out of karma, we step out of this labyrinth of life and reincarnation. We graduate. We evolve onto another plane of existence, closer to God, surely superior to life on earth. We don't stop living: we just live better. Definitely something worth working for.

What about those who are born wealthy or acquire great wealth? Are they experiencing good karma? Maybe not. As Martin Luther said: "The Lord God commonly grants riches to those gross asses to whom He vouchsafes nothing else."

In Luke, Jesus says: "How hardly shall they that have riches enter into the kingdom of God! For it is easier for a camel to go through a needle's eye, than for a rich man to enter into the kingdom of God." Having wealth is not necessarily bad. There are people who have great wealth and use it generously for the benefit of others. But being greedy is bad. Greed is selfishness and haughtiness. The selfish person assumes superiority over others. The assumption of superiority diminishes the soul, essentially making the haughty person less than, not more than. In seeing that person, we see someone who is on his way to God, as we all are, but is not at the point of evolution that his soul is ready to graduate to a higher plane. No, someone of lesser wealth, someone the greedy person would never trade places with, is the kind of person whose soul might be ready to ascend.

Success of the investment portfolio and success of the soul are two very different things. I recently heard someone refer to a young couple as being "very successful." Of course, that meant that they both make big money, have a house in a snooty neighborhood, drive unnecessarily extravagant cars and take trips to exotic places. They likely go to church—a very beautiful church full of expensively dressed people like themselves—and they probably wouldn't fit through the eye of a needle.

Let me tell you a success story. Shakespeare's contemporary, Christopher Marlowe, was a fine poet and playwright. We mentioned him before, as a pedophile. About two hundred years later he returned as Lord Byron, another noted poet. Byron's biography is full of excesses that complicated his own existence. He died young and returned as Oscar Wilde, yet another celebrated writer. There were more excesses, more complications, eventually landing him in prison for something that would merely make the gossip rags today. However, the prison experience broke his health, and he died early, ending a life shadowed by scandal. Wilde returned as the Welsh poet Dylan Thomas. The final stanza of his poem "Fern Hill" is a true gift to mankind. But in life Thomas was actually described as Byronic, and he died at 39 following an epic drinking spree. What did each of these incarnations have in common? Ramoth calls it self-sabotage. Each had enormous talent, each brought gifts to the world through writing, but each victimized himself through unfortunate decisions and thereby delayed his soul's advancement. Each man, despite fame, was a victim, not a student. However, Dylan Thomas came back. I know him now although he has no idea of his past lives. He doesn't write. He has done nothing to bring himself fame. He has worked diligently, bought a modest house, reared a family and acted charitably in his community. I doubt that many people envy him, but in this life, he is successful. He has broken the pattern of his previous lives, which swirled in an eddy of self-sabotage, and his soul has advanced. He is a greater man than the more famous men he has been.

A final fact about our souls is that they can exchange bodies. This sounds outlandish, but according to Ramoth it does occasionally happen. When a body gets a new soul, Ramoth refers to the phenomenon as a "walk-in." When I learned about walk-ins, I asked Ramoth if I was one. I was not, he said, but I knew someone who was. He asked me to identify someone who had undergone a significant personality change. After a while, I realized that I did know such a person. Over time a friend of mine had become increasingly morose, having no direction in life and seeming overwhelmed. He suffered a long, nasty bout of food poisoning and shortly after appeared to have rediscovered a purpose in life. I had indeed identified the correct person, Ramoth told me, adding that the walk-in had occurred during the illness. Walk-ins usually occur during a stressful event such as illness or injury.

A walk-in event allows a soul weary with life a chance to bail out while allowing another soul that has work to do on earth but does not need the childhood experience to step into a body. Often there is a pre-existing connection between the two souls. In my friend's case, his deceased great uncle stepped in. Interestingly, my friend eventually succumbed to the same disease that had claimed the great uncle. Also, Ramoth identified my friend's wife as the reincarnation of the great uncle's sweetheart, who died before they could marry. Perhaps, reuniting with her was the great uncle's impetus for walking in.

I asked Ramoth what effect the walk-in had on my friend's wife. "She knew something had happened, something good," he said. "She was delighted."

One method that helps me conceptualize the soul and some of its doings is to image that it's a person buying a brand-new car. The soul is the purchaser; the car is the body. I don't know anyone who has ever done this, but it is conceivable that a person might buy a new car and drive it for its entire lifetime, until it just doesn't have another mile to give. The driver abandons that car, so to speak. That represents the death of the body. The driver is just fine, though, and gets a new car. That's reincarnation. Another option is to drive the car for a few years and then sell it. When that happens, the driver passes the car to a new driver. From the car's perspective, that's a walk-in.

I learned that Franklin Roosevelt experienced a walk-in during the 1921 illness that permanently paralyzed his legs. Previously, he was another soul, but the FDR who guided America through the Great Depression and World War II was George Washington reincarnated. I learned also that I was busy being someone else in 1795 when John Keats was born. I walked in while he was still a child. I know of another case in which I walked into a young body. It happened in Italy following a near-drowning experience, when my soul, recently freed by execution from the body of John Wallace, stepped into the body that would grow to be Petrarch, the Italian Renaissance poet, reputed to be the first person known to have climbed a mountain for the sheer pleasure of doing so.

I actually walked into an older body shortly after spending 73 years in W.B. Yeats. According to Ramoth, in 1941, during the last few months of his life, I inhabited the body of American writer Sherwood Anderson for the express purpose of encouraging Anderson's friend Ernest Hemingway not to commit suicide. It must have worked, at least partially. Hemingway resisted killing himself for another twenty years. As for Anderson, a man with an impressive appetite for alcohol, he quaffed a martini so fast that he swallowed the toothpick, then with his wife boarded a passenger ship. The toothpick punctured the alimentary canal, with predictable results. At sea, not much could be done. The soul was freed.

Yvonne and I walked in together as a couple once, just briefly, and apparently in order to assure a particular outcome. In a regression she saw us bundled in furs, passengers in a horse-drawn sleigh moving urgently over snow to a great palace where some sort of ball was taking place. We were high-level prisoners, a king and queen, maybe, or at least nobles of some type. Guards led us into a room to await our "host," who appeared to be Peter the Great. When he arrived, he abruptly asked me if I was ready to meet his demands. I said: "Sir, you are a coward and a worm." He motioned. We were hustled into another room and quickly put to death. Yvonne believes that we walked into those lives just before they faced the tyrant so as to keep them from losing courage and caving in to his demands, whatever they were. What I find most interesting about the experience is that the expression "a coward and a worm" had been randomly popping into my mind for several years. After Yvonne's regression, though, it stopped.

Persistent but seemingly meaningless thoughts can be scraps of past lives coming to the surface, frequently because they are burdens that need to be examined and released. Sometimes things we feel drawn to do are connected to past lives. *Echoes from the Battlefield: First-Person Accounts of Civil War Past Lives* is a fascinating book by Dr. Barbara Lane. In it Dr. Lane discusses twelve case studies involving American Civil War re-enactors who submitted to hypnotic regression and discovered that they were reincarnations of Civil War soldiers. In the cases of these twelve, Lane was able to verify through research that the lives the men regressed to are historically authentic. Indeed, some of the re-enactors discovered that they were descendants of the lives they regressed to.

Through Ken I met Dr. Lane, who regressed me to the Civil War, the life of the Pearl Poet and Camelot. I already knew from Ramoth that I had been my own great-great-great uncle, a Confederate lieutenant. In the regression I was surprised to discover that I actually dressed like an officer, with a sword and a revolver. My men were one group among many, all feverishly digging a trench that overlooked a long, gentle slope. My heart broke for the men; I knew the war was a lost cause, and I knew that something terrible was soon to happen. We were near Spotsylvania Court House, Virginia. The thought of it upsets me even now. And oh, yes—within a few days all hell would break loose.

Ten

Karma and the Farm

For forty years I worked some land—meaning farmed—and for the last fifteen of those owned it, a property of a little over a hundred acres near a hamlet named Chamblissburg in Bedford County, Virginia. The property had originally been a 1,200-acre land grant from George II of England to an ancestor of mine named Carter. During the American Revolution, Carter sided with the colonists and changed his name to Carner, apparently to try to avoid any potential reprisal from the Crown. By the mid-1800s I believe the land had been whittled down to about 160 acres that belonged to a Carner daughter and her husband, a cobbler named Bradley. In the 1860s their three sons went to war.

Swept into Company K of the 58th Virginia Infantry were my great-great grandfather Robert Bradley and his brothers John Bradley and Monroe Bradley—actually Joseph Monroe Bradley. John Bradley was wounded in the arm at the Battle of Port Republic, near the campus of James Madison University, and evidently was discharged after that. During or immediately after the war, he left for Texas and was never heard from again. Robert Bradley fought until the Battle of Fredericksburg, where he was wounded in the thigh, which ended his involvement in the war. Both men were privates in the army. Their brother Monroe, however, was elected—yes, *elected*—first lieutenant. Their company commander was John Kasey, the same Kasey who is mentioned in my poem "Frank James Dreaming in Virginia." After the war Kasey would hold various official titles in Bedford County, including sheriff. The division commander was Jubal Early.

Monroe Bradley would die during the Battle of Spotsylvania Courthouse. On May 10, 1864, Union troops attacked a salient, or bulge, in the Confederate line, an area soon to be known as the "Mule Shoe," just about where Company K was positioned. In the fighting Monroe lost an ear. The next day was so rainy that there was no fighting, but on May 12 Grant sent a huge force against the salient once again. In the regression with Barbara Lane, I felt myself, sword in hand, leading my men forward to support the front. That's when I pitched forward, not dead but mortally wounded. Someone bent over me. I said: "Go on. I'll be all right."

Shortly after the regression with Barbara Lane, Yvonne and I drove to the battlefield, specifically to the site of the Mule Shoe. As we approached by car, we both felt a sense of oppression. So many men had died there, and so many others had had to see them die. May 12, 1864, is considered the single bloodiest day of the war. Down the road toward Richmond, at Yellow Tavern, Gen. J.E.B. Stuart died the same morning Monroe Bradley did. Just yards from where Monroe died is the concrete cast of a stump. That's where an oak tree roughly the diameter of a utility pole was shot down by musket fire.

Although partly filled in by time, the trench is still visible. About fifty yards behind it we found the spot where Monroe fell. I could see something like a shadow on the ground, sort of a silhouette of his body. Within it was a small rock. I still have that rock.

For months before our visit to Spotsylvania, I had suffered a stiff neck. On the right side of it, even the skin felt odd. I told Yvonne that it felt like a hand on my neck. Ramoth told me that the hand was a memory from the day of Monroe's death. He said that Union forces had driven the Confederates out of the trench and far beyond where Monroe lay, unable to move. That fact is verified by history. During that time, with the fighting quite distant, a union soldier moved among the wounded, trying to help those who couldn't hope to survive by breaking their necks. It was his hand that I felt on my neck. Probably the reason it still bothered me was that even with his neck broken, Monroe didn't die immediately.

As Yvonne and I wandered the unhappy scene, another person arrived—a powerful, long-haired young man on a bicycle. He dismounted and walked the area, almost aimlessly, as we probably seemed to. Then he rode away. One May 12 long ago, Ramoth said, he had been the man who tried to help Monroe by mercifully snapping his neck. He looked like a nice person.

I wrote this poem on the 135th anniversary of Monroe's death.

Monroe Bradley

First Lieutenant
Company K, 58th Virginia Infantry
KIA 12 May 1864
Spotsylvania Court House

I couldn't talk philosophy nor speak
great poetry, and I was much abashed
at times with proper officers from the
academies, for I was simple as
the crooked rows of corn we grew back home
and just that earnest in desire to stand,
and would have stayed that grounded in the soil
of my people's farm had not the war
uprooted everything and shucked me naked
to my nerves. Two days ago I pictured
what the sea is like—which I'd not seen—
when up into the salient we rushed
to swarm amid the swarm that Grant had stirred
against the crook in our thin line. I saw,
like water tiding up a beach, the waves
approach and falter on our volley, swell

and pour again, and in the noise and
the smoke that wet my eyes, the oddest thing—
I saw the storm they call a hurricane
that lashes oceans forward into towns;
I felt sea water seeping through a clapboard
wall and knew that momently a heave
would bash it in. But something in the riled
and shrieking air ripped through my ear, and I
remembered pain, and fought unthinking, fought
until the storm winds settled with the dusk.

Last night I heard the rain unequally
and felt uneasy quiet gnaw my wound,
and through the stench of dead men and the powder
smoke still dripping from the air and through
the scent of terror that had further soured
our sweat, I smelled the blood that wet the rag
around my head and saw my face upon
the ice pond at my home, with just one ear.
Coldly, as if I were someone else,
I wondered who would marry such a man
and wondered how the wind would whisper when
it gushed the narrow hollows of the farm
and if all voices there would seek one side
and if when talking with a friend, someday,
I'd cock my head and seem to look away.

When dawn came raining through the fog, and up
the slope the sea-swarm poured again, I rose,
my legs like lead, each arm a mushy log,
surprised to find my body such a load,
so worn that it was a relief amid
the clap and howl to feel a hailstone from
the soggy chill invite me to the mire,

where I could rest so tired I couldn't move,
where I could try to think of home but saw
a pine-and-honeysuckled hollow where
I crouched within the terror-laden sweat
of woolen clothes and heard teeth chattering
in warmth of May, some other May, somewhere,
some other where, where I was learning, even
then, where I was learning life is heavy,
rest is easy, it is hard to breathe.

Monroe Bradley died on May 12, 1864. One year, one month and one day later, on June 13, 1865, William Butler Yeats was born in Ireland. He lived until January 28, 1939. Fourteen years and fourteen days later, I was born. Those numbers must mean something. A few years ago, I purchased a cell phone and was randomly issued a number that ended in "0613"—Yeats's birthday. Unfortunately, I lost the phone, and when I bought a new phone, the company wouldn't let me keep the old number.

By war's end, Robert Bradley got the farm. John headed for Texas, disappearing into the big sunset. Monroe's body came home and settled into the dust, the grave's location lost in time. A new generation inherited the land, and another after that. Then a large chunk of it came to my parents, and I began working the best acreage, cultivating Christmas trees. After my mother died, my father deeded the property to Yvonne and me, and we moved onto it and turned it into a horse farm. In terms of karma, the farm boy-turned-lieutenant had come home at last.

According to Ramoth, before the war Monroe had wanted to court a girl named Molly, who shared aspects with Yvonne. Monroe went to her father, a preacher, to ask permission to see the girl. Permission was denied. It seems that Monroe had bought books for black children and helped them learn to read. It's probably good that the preacher didn't know the whole story. According to Ramoth, as young as he was, Monroe had become part of the Underground Railroad, hiding runaway slaves somewhere on the farm and helping them make their way north. I've often wondered at the irony that such a man could also be an officer in the Confederate army.

The American Civil War caused several souls who had been in Camelot to choose sides and fight. Lincoln had been Galahad. Grant had been a knight in Camelot and later would be Harry S. Truman. George McClellan had been Sir Tor, the knight who dispatched Gawain. George Custer had been Sir Bedevere and would later be Ezra Pound, the American poet. On the Southern side, we already know that Gawain became an obscure minor officer. Bors, who had been William the Conqueror and Robert the Bruce—as well as George Washington—was James Longstreet. Tuck was Stonewall Jackson, and Sir Kay—who had been Napoleon and would later be George Patton—was John Kasey, Monroe Bradley's company commander. Monroe's division commander, Jubal Early, had been Percival, Miles Standish, George II of England and a Cherokee mystic whose name translates to Dawn Running; he would become the World War I Irish pilot Robert Gregory (lauded by Yeats in the poem "An Irish Airman Foresees His Death") and the American football player John Unitas. While I have never confirmed his existence in Camelot, J.E.B. Stuart had already been important in American history as Capt. John Smith, of Jamestown fame, and Patrick Henry. Lee had been Hannibal, Lancelot, William Wallace and Lafayette and would return as Dwight D. Eisenhower.

History is indeed prologue. The present is a reflection of the past. Cycles continue until they're broken. We'll choose sides and kill one another until we become students of the cycle itself—and change it. Maybe an understanding of reincarnation will help us do that. How long have the above-mentioned combatants been busy slaying one another? I don't know, but let's take a look at the Trojan War. They've been at it at least since then.

Eleven

The Trojan Horse

Homer's *The Iliad* is a marvelous piece of work. A classic epic poem, it's written in 24 books, which would correspond to chapters in a modern novel. The cast of characters is huge, and Homer presents his story so objectively that we could argue forever whether he favors the Trojans or the Achaeans (Greeks). *The Iliad* is essentially the story of a personal dispute that takes place within the greater conflict known as the Trojan War. The two conflicts are parallel: in each, one man has taken a woman from another man.

Yes, someone is thinking, *but* The Iliad *is a made-up story. If the Trojan War did happen, surely the characters and particulars of the story are fiction.* Ramoth's answer to that is that most stories from the ancient world are based on real events and real people. There are fictional aspects, of course, but at least in the case of this epic, the primary characters did exist, and most are reincarnating even today.

In the back-story to *The Iliad,* the Trojans strike the first blow—or rather, one Trojan prince does something politically stupid. On a diplomatic visit to Sparta, Paris—son of the Trojan king, Priam—steals Helen from her husband Menelaus, who happens to be the Spartan king. Although this is viewed as an abduction, Helen is in love with Paris and leaves with him willingly. Menelaus and his brother Agamemnon, a more powerful king, put together what today is called a coalition army from all surrounding city-states and sail in a thousand ships to Asia Minor to retrieve the stolen Helen. Let's not be naïve enough to believe that all those city-states are after justice for Menelaus. Troy and its surrounding city-states are very wealthy. As usual, the primary factor in this war is greed.

The Iliad begins near the end of the war and ends before the war is over. It focuses on the conflict between the Achaeans' supreme commander, Agamemnon, and his greatest warrior, Achilles. Briefly, Achilles has a young woman, Briseis, whom he has acquired as a war prize, and Agamemnon takes her for himself. (Remember, it was taking someone else's girl that started the war.) Predictably upset, Achilles goes on strike, refusing to fight for Agamemnon or let the soldiers under him fight.

Meanwhile, the Achaean and Trojan armies clash continually, with the Trojans gaining an advantage. Patroclus, Achilles's friend since childhood, surreptitiously dons Achilles's armor and, posing as Achilles, leads the army into battle. The Trojan prince Hector, Troy's greatest hero, slays Patroclus. To avenge his friend, Achilles challenges Hector to a one-on-one battle. Knowing that he cannot defeat Achilles, Hector accepts—and dies.

This extremely brief summary takes us approximately to the end of *The Iliad*. Centuries after Homer, Quintas of Smyrna (also known as Quintas Smyrnaeus) wrote *The Fall of Troy*, which begins where Homer's epic ends and concludes with the sack of Troy. Quintas's portrayal of the surviving characters is consistent with Homer's. Aside from the inclusion of gods and goddesses, both works are surprisingly accurate, according to Ramoth. And they involve real souls.

First, the femme fatale, Helen. Yeats wrote many poems about Maud Gonne in which he referred to her as Helen of Troy, supposedly the most beautiful woman ever but the bringer of heartache and destruction. (Christopher Marlowe, writing of Helen, asks: "Is this the face that launched a thousand ships?") Yeats got it right. I have no idea whether he believed that Maud had been Helen or he simply used Helen as a very apt symbol for Maud, but he got it right. Maud really had been Helen.

There are other women in the Trojan War story, but two have been identified by Ramoth. Agamemnon's wife, Clytemnestra, murders him in his bath when he returns home from the war. She shows up in Camelot as Guinevere. The Trojan princess Cassandra is a priestess and psychic who knows that the Trojan Horse needs to be burned rather than treated as a gift from the Achaeans. It is, of course, filled with the Achaean soldiers who sack and destroy Troy. Unsurprisingly, in Camelot she returns as Marrion and today is Yvonne.

Among the Achaean men let's consider Agamemnon, Achilles, Patroclus, Diomedes, Nestor and Ajax, son of Telemon. In Camelot, Agamemnon was Arthur, Achilles was Bors, Patroclus was Mordred, and Diomedes was Lancelot. Nestor, who was old and no longer a fighter but was important for his wisdom and advice, in Camelot was Tuck. Ajax, son of Telemon, also known as Ajax the Greater so as not to be confused with another character named Ajax, was Gawain in Camelot, although not in full. Gawain possessed aspects of Ajax. And Odysseus? From the first time I read *The Iliad*, while I was drawn to Ajax, I found Odysseus distasteful and dishonorable, and I positively dislike *The Odyssey*, which depicts him as a great hero. Maybe there's a karmic reason. In Camelot, Odysseus was Merlin.

The Trojan hero Hector became Perceval in Camelot. Hector's father, King Priam, was Arthur's brother. I believe his name was Uthergard and, according to Ramoth, he was skilled in all aspects of horsemanship and oversaw Arthur's stables.

Let's consider something interesting about Priam and Hector. Throughout his writings, Homer uses what scholars call "Homeric epithets," little descriptive phrases that he attaches to the names of characters, often using the same epithet repeatedly with a particular name. Examples include "great man-slaughtering Achilles," "Diomedes of the great war cry" and "Zeus the cloud gatherer." When referring to any Trojan male, he is likely to use the epithet "a breaker of horses," sometimes translated as "a tamer of horses." This tells us that the Trojans are known for their horsemanship. Having been around horses for years and knowing that breaking or taming horses is one thing and actually using them is another thing entirely, I wonder if Homer really meant "a master of horses." If you'll allow me to use my own term, then, Priam and Hector are both "masters of horses." Notice that Priam, as Uthergard, was in charge of Arthur's horses.

In my present life the Priam-Uthergard soul was my own maternal grandfather. Long before I knew about that, though, and shortly after beginning my studies with Ramoth, during meditation I saw a vision of my grandfather sitting on the steps to the side porch of the house he grew up in, which I visited occasionally as a child. A few feet from him grazed the sorrel pony my parents had bought when I was a small boy. The symbolism of that vision—my grandfather watching over my little horse—would have to wait several years to become apparent to me. He was still a master of horses.

I find it interesting that in some of Hector's future lives the epithet "master of horses" takes on a more elaborate meaning. As Gen. Jubal Early in the American Civil War, he committed a war crime in Hagerstown, Maryland, by robbing the town's bank and turning the loot over to the Confederate treasury. That created a karmic debt. Not all karmic debts are misery to repay, however. As the football quarterback John Unitas, he at first had some trouble getting established with a team but eventually joined the Baltimore Colts. Arguably the greatest football player of his time, Johnny Unitas brought happiness, pride and income to the state of Maryland. And what team did he play for? The Colts. As the quarterback was he not once again a master of horses? In the final year of his career, Unitas played for the San Diego Chargers. The Chargers were known for the lightning bolt depicted on their helmets, possibly making one think that the team's name has something to do with electricity, but the word "charger" is a name for a war horse. I submit that the idea that there is meaning here is more logical than to believe that we're looking at compounded coincidences. This is a real pattern, and each part of it is a clue. Such clues are all around us all the time, but most of us earthlings haven't yet learned to look for them. God is trying to tell us something.

Now let's add a layer to the story of the Trojan War with information from Ramoth, specifically concerning Ajax and Cassandra. According to legend, prior to the sack of Troy, Ajax the Greater loses a wrestling match to Odysseus and shortly after kills the Achaeans' sheep and commits suicide. Ramoth's story is different. According to him, before the Trojan War as a prince himself, Ajax spent considerable time in Priam's court, enough time to fall in love with Priam's daughter Cassandra. The two wanted to marry, which would have created a good diplomatic tie between two city-states. Ajax and some of Priam's many sons were good friends. A particularly strong bond formed between Ajax and Hector, likely because they were both gifted soldiers and natural leaders. Ajax entered the war only because of duty, and he fought well. Homer describes him as the Achaeans' second-greatest warrior, behind only Achilles. Longing for Cassandra and certainly not hating his enemies, Ajax considered changing sides. When I pointed out to Ramoth that Homer depicts Ajax and Hector fighting one-on-one for an entire day, he agreed that they did, but no blood spilled between them and at end of day they embraced and went their separate ways, which Homer does depict. Arms had clashed, yes, but more importantly, they had spent the day talking.

Through Yvonne, Ramoth once regressed me to the life of Ajax. Unlike in some regressions, I didn't see myself as if I were standing nearby; I saw through Ajax's eyes. I was outdoors, seated on something. Ramoth instructed me to look down. I saw big, square feet and stocky, hairy legs. I was looking at the lower body of a huge man, just as Homer described Ajax. The index finger of the right hand was missing.

"There's a scar on your cheek where the beard doesn't grow," Ramoth said. "You are very tired of war. Now see yourself in battle."

I found myself on the front row of a phalanx facing an enemy phalanx. My comrades and I stood so close together that our shields touched. We literally pushed our shields against the shields of the Trojans, and as we jabbed with spears, Trojan spears jabbed at us. We ducked behind our shields to avoid being stabbed. I neither injured nor was injured, nor did I see anyone injured, but in the regression I stayed in that setting only for a few seconds. It was no place to linger.

I was able to return to the life of Ajax through regression, which implies that I likely possess a major aspect of him. The soul of anyone who lived as far back as Ajax is likely to have been spread pretty far and wide, to have been shared among many souls—or maybe not. As distant from my present life as Gawain was, Ramoth says that I'm a full reincarnation of him.

Weary and hopeless, Ramoth told me, Ajax performed a solitary rite in which he sacrificed sheep, then killed himself, hoping to purchase Cassandra's safety by offering himself to the gods. Just think what an ancient Greek playwright could have done with that.

Most of us know that the Trojan War ended when Odysseus devised the plan to build a gigantic wooden horse meant to appear to honor those masters of horses, the Trojans. The Achaeans would leave the horse outside Troy's gate, then sail their thousand ships toward home. Presumably, the Trojans would consider the horse a peace offering from a retiring Achaean army, bring the horse inside the city and celebrate victory over Agamemnon until they were marvelously drunk. All went according to plan. Achaean soldiers poured from the belly of the horse, Achaean ships returned to the shore, bringing all the soldiers who couldn't fit inside the horse, and Troy fell immediately—like Camelot. The Achaeans destroyed the city, hauled away its wealth and the most nubile of its women and laid waste to a civilization. Like Camelot's, Troy's fall was brought about chiefly by the Odysseus-Merlin soul.

I asked Ramoth what happened to the surviving Trojans. They became the Celts, he answered. That's a big answer. The Celts, also known as the Goths, swept across Europe, settling as far west as Ireland. They were a fierce, warlike people. Among other accomplishments, they sacked Rome in 410 CE.

According to one line of thought, they actually founded Rome. The Trojan leader Aeneas, a distant cousin of Hector, led a group of refugees to the Italian peninsula and created a new civilization where Rome stands today. As theories go, that story is more plausible than the one about Romulus and Remus, the twin infants who were reared by a wolf. Also, there is a belief that a descendant of Aeneas, Brute of Troy, led a contingent of former Trojans to Britain, which offers an explanation for the Celtic presence in the British Isles.

William Butler Yeats probably would have had no particular reason to connect Brute with the Celts, but he surely would have known about Brute and his connection to the Trojans. Perhaps he alludes to that obliquely in a poem I mentioned earlier, "Leda and the Swan."

In this fourteen-line poem, a sonnet, Yeats first describes the attack in which Zeus, in the form of a swan, rapes the Spartan queen Leda. The offspring from this attack will include Helen and Clytemnestra—Helen of Troy and the Clytemnestra who marries and then murders Agamemnon. In lines nine, ten and half of eleven, Yeats tells us that the union will bring about Troy's destruction and Agamemnon's death. Then he asks if Leda "put on [Zeus's] knowledge with his power" before Zeus "let her drop" and went on about his godly business. The "power" that Yeats refers to is the power of destruction, which passes through Leda on its way to her daughters and through them to Troy and Agamemnon. The word "knowledge" implies even more, that Zeus's deliberate purpose in raping Leda is to bring about Troy's destruction in order to remake the world, partly by establishing Rome and Britain. Of course, the poem is also an expression of the misery Maud Gonne—or his obsession with her—has brought into the poet's life. In Yeats's poems, any mention of Helen is also a reference to Maud.

As I took you through these historical episodes, we've looked at something that reminds me of theater—the same troupe of actors playing different roles in dramas just different enough. Troy, Camelot, the Civil War, William Wallace's insurrection—even Roland's battle and the Norman Conquest—all follow a pattern suggesting the cycles of history and human behavior that need to be broken before we can become something more than we are and what we have been. The souls who keep participating in these dramas have likely been together for millennia. Some of them, possibly all—Ramoth included, he told me—were among the Israelites who fled from Egypt. Some, possibly all, interacted with Jesus of Nazareth. Ramoth himself met Him in Greece prior to the three years of teaching and healing recorded in the four gospels.

The seed from which each of these struggles grew—apparently from which all human struggles grow—is greed. It causes war, death, pestilence—the list goes on. Greed, therefore, must be the greatest sin of all. It causes other sins.

Ramoth once told me that those where he resides marvel at the fact that we on earth think gold is so important. Another puzzling human idea, he said to me, is that having more than enough is better than simply having enough. Evidently greed doesn't permeate the universe. It's a human affliction. Need creates greed, and greed creates need. That's a cycle—one we've been stuck in for a long, long time. What would happen if we broke that cycle? Put this book down and think about it.

Twelve

Aliens

In one of my earliest meetings with Ramoth, I asked about extraterrestrials—did they exist, and was earth being visited by them? Yes, they exist, Ramoth explained, and earth has been visited by them since before the time of recorded history. He referred to two types of aliens, the Pleiadeans and the Zetas, also called the Grays.

The Pleiadeans, he continued, are spiritual, highly-evolved people who serve God and bring a great love for mankind. In the past they've influenced events on earth, always to our benefit and in accordance with God's wishes. People who see Pleiadeans often mistake them for angels because of their physical beauty and their kind demeanor, and they can communicate with us telepathically. They come from the star group called the Pleiades, which is over 400 light-years from us in the constellation Taurus. Pleiadeans who visit earth travel through wormholes in order to by-pass the great distance, spend one earth year here and then travel home. When they arrive home, the people they left behind have aged a great deal, far more than the travelers themselves. It's a huge commitment for a Pleiadean to visit earth. Ramoth told me that I'd seen a female Pleiadean once, sitting on my bed. That was the beautiful woman I'd woken to when I was very small.

We will never have anything to fear from the Pleiadeans. Ramoth says it is possible for earthlings to evolve into Pleiadeans. Life among them doesn't involve the pettiness and violence that so often come with earthly life.

The Grays, however, were on earth when Ramoth taught me about them, but they're gone from here now, although they are still at large somewhere in the universe. They're generally bad aliens and according to Ramoth were not created by God. They were developed as living artificial intelligence by a race of people on a planet in the Zeta Reticuli star system in the constellation Reticulum, about 39 light-years from us. The creatures got out of hand and destroyed their creators. Their planet had two suns, Ramoth said. Temperatures on the planet began rising, for whatever reason, and the Grays realized that they had to move. Earth was still a bit warm for their liking, and the atmospheric composition wasn't perfect, but it would do. The Grays came to earth around the mid-1800s and established bases underground and underwater as well as on both the moon and Mars.

The Grays have no souls and no emotions. They are biological computers that could live for about 150 years under optimum conditions on their original planet, and like the Pleiadeans can communicate with us telepathically. They look just like we think they look from drawings, cartoons and toys, but people who imagine the Grays as cute, sweet little E.T.s are like people who think Merlin was a loveable old wizard.

Much about the Grays is ominous. If they could destroy their creators, surely they could do the same to us, but they didn't, and now they won't. God interceded. We'll get to that.

Grays' heads resemble the heads of ants, and their behavior is also ant-like. There are what we might call worker Grays and a leader Gray who telepathically commands his underlings and is actually larger and looks different from other Grays, with twice the lifespan. Take away the leader, and the worker Grays can't survive long. They don't know what to do.

Certain species of ants actually make something like herd animals of aphids. Similarly, somewhere in their explorations, the Grays came upon a race of bi-pedal reptilian-like beings that were intelligent enough to be useful. The Grays and the reptilians formed a symbiotic relationship, but the Grays who came to earth didn't bring reptilians with them. According to Ramoth, there have been no reptilian aliens present on earth.

The strikingly consistent idea of Grays, what they look like and where they came from supports the idea that they really did contact and communicate with human beings. Also, they were adept at using holography, projecting three-dimensional images of themselves, their spacecrafts and presumably their reptilian allies, much to the terror of our friends and neighbors.

My own friend John was once camping near Dolly Sods, West Virginia, an area formerly known as a hot-spot for UFO activity, when he woke in the night to see a Gray standing at the door of his tent. Unable to move, John stared in alarm at the creature. I was present when he spoke to Ramoth about the event.

"It might have been 30 seconds or 30 minutes that I was frozen there," he said. "I had no sense of time."

"It was 36 minutes," Ramoth said. "But the creature you saw wasn't real. It was a projection."

Even so, it was real enough that John, who is not a faint-hearted man, was frozen in place. However, being unable to move in the presence of Grays is not necessarily due to fear alone. They seemed able sometimes to control the minds of people and even animals. More about that later.

In the early 1990s Yvonne had several interactions with the Grays, specifically with a powerful leader. Getting out of her car, she saw a Gray standing on her porch roof. Because she could see *through* the Gray, she realized that it was a holographic projection, which was only a slight comfort. The image wore gray trousers and a gray shirt, with a sash that crossed one shoulder. On the sash were seven stars. The projection identified himself as Athor, leader of the Grays. The name Athor sounds suspiciously like something from a comic book; even the clothing is like a parody of an earthly military uniform. However, Ramoth uses the name Athor to identify this Gray and sees him as a real entity, not just a three-dimensional cartoon.

Athor wanted Yvonne to give him her infant son and expected her to do so simply because Athor was an alien and Yvonne was supposed to be in terror. Indeed, she was startled, but she also had Ramoth's guidance. She refused the request and told the interstellar creep to be gone.

Athor came back, appearing in Yvonne's bedroom. Same request, same results. The third time, Athor was more insistent. Instead of appearing in her room, he caused the bed to levitate several feet, with Yvonne lying awake on it. Then he let it fall. After that, he gave up the quest. Yvonne would hear from Athor again, though.

We've all heard of people being abducted by the Grays. During the 1990s I knew several people who believed they had been abducted. The Grays attempted to abduct me several times, but Ramoth had forewarned me and told me what to do to thwart them. We used to hear about people having small metallic objects implanted in their bodies and of doctors sometimes finding and removing them. The Grays were definitely up to something. They had a big problem, and they were trying to solve it.

During the 1900s the Gray females all became barren, possibly due to living in earth's unfamiliar environment. Whether because female Grays served only to reproduce or for some other reason, the males destroyed them. At that point the Grays' continued survival lay in creating a cross-race with human beings.

According to Ramoth, Grays are essentially mammals, with DNA close enough that they could produce offspring with human beings. The infant might or might not get a soul through the human parent. Hybrids, however, are barren, which led to much experimentation by the Grays. Thorough researchers, the Grays attempted hybridization with all of the human races. As it turned out, the darker the human skin, the less human the complexion of the hybrid appeared, so Caucasians became the preferred genetic partners.

If one moves in the right (or wrong) circle, one is likely to meet a person who proudly claims to be descended from the Grays. Remember, Gray hybrids are infertile, so if the individual claims to have a Gray grandparent or has a child of her own, she is full of hot air. Similarly, Ramoth explained, since nowhere in the universe can a reptile cross with a mammal, anyone claiming a Reptilian relative is—well, mistaken.

When Ramoth first spoke to me about the Grays, he told me that I had once met a female Gray hybrid, revealing approximately where I'd met her and leaving it to me to remember the incident. Several months passed before I recalled it, and then I was surprised that I took so long because the woman's appearance was quite unique. I was 18 when some business brought me into her office. I thought she was at least ten years older than I. She was a small-boned, thin, personable individual. The odd thing about her was her nose. She almost didn't have one. Between her eyes was a flat surface. Halfway between her eyes and her mouth a bit of a nose climbed from her face, just enough to give her nostrils. When I met her, I assumed that she had a birth defect and felt sorry for her—but never quite forgot that peculiar face or her name, even.

In the late 1990s Ramoth identified for me one friend after another who had been implanted by the Grays. The implants allowed the aliens to keep track of people and also to influence their thoughts, thus their actions. Many of my students were implanted, he said. My observation at the time was that more students than ever made absent-minded mistakes—forgetting to submit an essay on time, not proofreading, failing to perform assignments, being unprepared for quizzes.

John mentioned to me that a fight with the Grays was coming and that Ramoth had told him he had a part to play in it. I asked Ramoth about that, and he said that I had a part to play, too, if I would accept it. Like many of us, I'd been scared of aliens since I was a little boy, but this wasn't just a guy from down the street inviting me to join the National Guard. This was Ramoth, an emissary from God. I had to say yes.

The Grays, Ramoth explained, intended to experiment until they produced a race of beings who could replace their own race, then to destroy the rest of humanity and take our planet for their own. They would use disease to kill us all, Ramoth said. Meanwhile, they would continue taking people from among us, sometimes not just for implantation but for terrifying, cruel, fatal experimentation. Those unfortunate individuals were among the folks who disappear and are never heard from again.

John and I both imagined ourselves with assault rifles blasting away at ray gun-wielding Grays and probably dying in the process. We never guessed that we would face the aliens using Old Testament-era technology.

Yvonne normally came into town every other weekend to give private readings and to hold a group meeting on Saturday evenings. Ramoth suggested to her that she begin holding a Sunday-morning meeting for a smaller group of invited people. It took several months for the makeup of the group to stabilize, but John, Ken, Leslie and I were always members. Eventually, Yvonne and the four of us comprised the group as others dropped out.

Ramoth referred to us as the Star, each of us representing one point. In time it would be the Star members who traveled to England, but we had other business first. As the Star we learned much about our past lives together as well as many historical and spiritual things. Ramoth instructed us on a level that he deemed inappropriate for Yvonne's regular group meetings, which brought together people from all stages of spiritual growth as well as the occasional scoffer. He also taught us much about the Grays. We needed to know all we could learn. We five were to be the warriors. Actually, there would be one other—

William Wallace, but he would be there only in spirit. Ramoth linked John, Ken and me most strongly to our Camelot lives—Bors, Tuck and Gawain—but William was always identified as the Scottish freedom fighter and never as Lancelot. It took us quite a while to realize that this was because William was ashamed of his traitorous role as Lancelot in Camelot.

Meanwhile, in automatic writing I got this sentence: "The Ark of the Covenant was a powerful generator." When I asked Ramoth about the sentence, he said it was time for John, Ken and me to start building an ark to use against the Grays. The three of us got together and realized that each had received information spiritually. When we put the information together, we had our plan for the ark.

The ark would be a cubic wooden box, 30 inches in each dimension, as I recall. We would use wood from four species, one for each of us, William included. William wanted maple, we learned. John chose walnut, Ken oak and I dogwood. We readily purchased maple, walnut and oak boards but could find no dogwood. I went into the forest behind where I grew Christmas trees, found a dogwood tree, and cut it. Dogwoods are small trees, so we decided to use my wood as trim for the box. Ken had received the idea that the top of the box should be a four-sided pyramid covered with mirrored glass. Inside, the box would be lined with leather.

Ken lived well secluded in the country, and we went to work in his basement garage, meeting every Wednesday after dinner. Among other things, John was a carpenter. Ken and I were something less, but the three of us worked together well. Nevertheless, work was slow. For a small box, the ark had a fairly complex design, and to make matters worse, we suffered one complication after another. We used John's professional grade table saw, and even though we carefully set the saw to cut a particular depth or width, on some nights the adjustments would not stay put. By the time we ran a single board through the saw, the settings would change, and the board would be ruined. The Grays knew we were doing something, and they didn't like it. How they readjusted the settings, we didn't know.

They played havoc with electrical instruments, too. During the period when we worked on the ark, John got into his car one morning to find that much of the vehicle's wiring had been burned to the point of uselessness, requiring a major rewiring job. One morning I found that all the radio settings in my car had been changed. No damage had been done, but I understood it as a message. The late 1990s was still the era of VCRs—videotapes. Yvonne tried to watch a tape on the subject of aliens, but her VCR machine died, its wiring frazzled. She bought a new machine and tried again. The same thing happened.

One night after working on the ark, Ken, John and I walked out of Ken's garage to find ourselves in an opaque, unnatural darkness. We couldn't see each other. It was like being deep in a cave. Ken returned to the garage and brought out a flashlight so John and I could get in our cars and leave. Once we got away from Ken's house, the sky became normal. On a different night, Leslie experienced the same eerie darkness. None of us had ever known anything like it.

Driving home from Ken's place one night, I absently turned off the main road onto a dark, narrow, poorly paved road that seemed to lead toward nothing good. Suspecting that the Grays had influenced me to take that road, I searched for a place to turn around. When I found a place to do so, in the dark I backed the car's rear wheels into a ditch at the pavement's edge. I couldn't pull forward. Fighting panic, I surrounded myself with light, left the car in neutral, got out and surveyed the problem—all while searching the sky and surroundings for signs of Grays. Fortunately, my car, a Mazda Miata, was much lighter than average, and even though I wasn't very big or especially strong, I lifted the rear of the car and pushed until the wheels sat on pavement. Then I made haste toward home.

(I think I might have gotten a little help lifting the car. Once when Ken and I struggled to move a heavy sofa up a flight of stairs, just at the point that our combined strength faltered, we both felt the sofa get lighter, and we mounted the stairs with it.)

Another evening, after driving home from a late class at the college, I got out of the car and started toward the house. Suddenly I stopped, confused and seemingly unable or unwilling to walk. With great effort I thought. *It's the Grays*, I told myself. *Use light.* As I had on the lonely road, I mentally surrounded myself with God's white light. Immediately the fogginess of my mind and body lifted, and I hurried into the house. And locked the door, not that it would help.

Even inside the house I wasn't wholly protected from the Grays' influence. I woke one night finding myself confused and unable to move except to breathe. I fought the confusion and regained movement. I had heard of sleep paralysis but had never experienced anything like it. Also, even though the experience shared some qualities with a nightmare, I emerged from it without the usual results of a nightmare—rapid heart rate, heavy breathing and fright. Ramoth later explained that the Grays had attempted to abduct me. If it happened again, I was to call for Jesus.

Eventually it did happen again. When I woke and couldn't move, I called mentally for Jesus, and the experience immediately ended. Once again, even though this time I woke believing I was being abducted by aliens, when it was over I felt none of the symptoms of a nightmare.

The next time it happened was worse. In what I took to be a dream, I was in deep snow wrestling someone I couldn't see. I woke, unable to move and barely able to think. I struggled to remember what I needed to do. When I called for Jesus, I heard screeching. Ramoth said that I'd actually been *inside* a spacecraft and that the white I remembered was the craft's interior. Abduction, he said, involved a *Star Trek*-like teleportation. That was the last time I ever had such an experience.

However, I had another experience in my house, which Ramoth attributed to the Grays and which showed me that they had a way of spying on people inside their homes. I had been reading a book about how to speak Cherokee in which I learned that there are no "M" sounds in the Cherokee language. After meditating, I began automatic writing and soon was getting a message from someone who identified herself as a Cherokee princess. Her name, however, began with an M. I stopped writing immediately.

During the fall before we built the ark, the Grays actually landed a short distance from my house, Ramoth told me, adding that they could get no closer to me. At about that time, they did the same near Ken's house. Ramoth told him where to look, and later Ken showed me a crushed patch of pokeberry plants at the edge of his yard. We laughed imagining a flying saucer zooming into the night sky, its bottom half speckled with purple stains.

The aliens threw some punches—some pretty scary ones, in fact—but the three ark builders managed a counterpunch one night. As we stood outside the garage after finishing the night's work, one of us noticed a light like a star moving in the sky. As we all watched, it made a right-angle turn. Airplanes, helicopters and satellites don't do that. Drones can, perhaps, but the year was 2000, and the light appeared to be quite high as well as silent. Ramoth had told us that we could disable the Grays' crafts by sending them light. The three of us concentrated on sending God's white light to the UFO. It stopped moving and moved no more. We would later hear evidence that we knocked it out of commission.

So week after week, we worked to complete the ark, a wooden box with a mirrored top. What would go in the box was as important as the box itself. Let's discuss my part of the contents, beginning with the back-story.

Early in my studies with Ramoth, he spoke to me about the power of crystals and various stones in general. Quartz crystals, especially, have an ability to transmit and receive energy. Because crystals both absorb and emit energy, I was told that whenever I acquired a crystal, I should cleanse it of all energy not my own by soaking it in a container of salt water for 24 hours. The salt crystals, I presume, absorb whatever energy the quartz has previously acquired. Then I needed to handle the crystal myself to align its energy with mine. I believe this power is real, and here's why.

Following instructions, I bought a length of copper pipe from the plumbing section of a hardware store, plus a copper cap to fit over the end of the pipe. Then I got some soft leather, from which I cut a strip about two inches wide and maybe two feet long. After cutting a section of copper pipe to about a foot in length, I fitted a quartz point—a single, elongated quartz crystal that comes to a point on one end—into the short copper pipe, with the pointed end of the quartz aiming outward. Using pliers, I crimped the pipe around the quartz as best I could. Then I capped the other end of the pipe and wrapped its length in leather, using a little glue. I had a wand.

I held the wand when I meditated so as to charge it with my energy. I believe the wand was simply a way of directing my energy, focusing and perhaps concentrating it. Ramoth warned me not to point it at myself because it could give me a headache. I obeyed that warning for a few days, but eventually I couldn't resist. I pointed the wand at my chest. Immediately I felt a pressure permeate my thorax.

One morning I got out of bed and stepped on a bumblebee. A bumblebee's sting is intense. I felt pain all the way to my knee. I sat in a chair and focused the wand on the site of the sting. Within a minute the pain was gone—literally gone. The sting did cause swelling, but the swelling was never painful. I don't know how or why using a wand ended the pain, but I do know that it ended.

Ramoth told me that a small crystal is as powerful as a large crystal. I purchased a quartz cluster that featured a dozen or more crystals all connected and was small enough to sit on my palm. In automatic writing I got that I could increase the power of the cluster 10,000 times. Semantically, to increase something 10,000 times is not the same as multiplying it by 10,000; it might mean to increase it by tiny increments 10,000 times. When I asked Ramoth if the message was valid, he said that it was and that I should interpret the wording to mean 10,000-fold. The process would take a year, though. The first step would be to take the cluster and a small wooden cross to the back section of my parents' farm, which was wooded and rose to the crest of a small mountain. I would go to the exact spot where the cluster should be buried just beneath the surface. I was to drive the cross into the ground next to the crystals. This needed to be done on the day of the next full moon. "You will see a great bird," Ramoth said.

On the day of the full moon, I headed to the farm, hoping to see a bald eagle fly overhead. Once I got into the woods, though, my attention focused on finding an exact spot that I had no description of and no directions to. Eventually I stopped at a place that just felt right. I buried the quartz and planted the cross. Only then did I think about the great bird. I glanced upward—and broke into laughter. From exactly where I stood, a contorted tree limb created the illusion of a large bird perched directly above me. All it took was one step in any direction to destroy the illusion. In a big forest I'd found the right spot, exactly.

The entire project involved creating a medicine wheel, like some Native Americans did. The nucleus of the wheel was a large rock on the mountain's crest, which I had already identified as a special object, a site of high energy. Each full moon I would retrieve the cluster, move it to its next location, bury it and place another wooden cross next to it. As I did this, the quartz cluster would increase in power, and at the same time I would help "balance" the energy of the farm, which someday would be my home, Ramoth said.

Full moon followed full moon, and I tried to move the quartz cluster geometrically around the big rock using my poor math skills and a compass, but it was difficult because of the rugged terrain and the fact that one can't see far in an Appalachian forest. About three full moons into the project, though, I found myself confused in the woods, with the compass needle sweeping around the dial like the second hand of a watch. I had to put the compass away and wander until I found a spot that felt right. When I spoke with Ramoth next, he told me that the compass had been influenced by the Grays, who were keeping an eye on my activities in the woods and were trying to cause me confusion. Following Ramoth's advice, on the full moons that followed, I entered the forest with a small mirror atop my head, held in place by a ball cap. The mirror would deflect the energy the aliens aimed at me. I readily admit that it's creepy to be alone in the forest with reason to believe that aliens are watching and don't like what you're doing.

Within a few months it became obvious that the big stone wasn't the geometric center of the medicine wheel, which itself was starting to be more an uneven loop than a circle. When I reported this to Ramoth, he assured me that geometric perfection was unimportant to the wheel's function. He reminded me that I'd been led to exactly the correct spot beneath the great bird and asked why I believed I hadn't been led to the correct spot every full moon since then. I wrote a poem to help me remember that message.

Nature's Circles

Nature's circles run wilder than ours,
to heaven perfect, to us flawed—
vexing homilies of poorly drawn loops,
pipefitters' banes bent out of round,
objects and accidents, winds and floods
that refuse to fit our plans.

Allowed to pick its path, sometimes
the mystic's medicine wheel won't close
without a wobble in its arc,
commending all forms we can't control—
like anyone's face, not quite halved
by a line down the middle,

or heaven's prophets, smudged with error,
forgetful, bewildered, yet leaning toward home.

Perhaps a year before the medicine wheel project began, an object came into my mind—a symbol, I thought, for the new age following the Second Coming. Ramoth encouraged me to construct the symbol, which I called a new age cross. In explaining it to John, I used the expression "two-dimensional pyramid," which he understood immediately. It's a square with diagonal lines running from corner to opposite corner, crossing in the exact center, where Ramoth said a quartz crystal should be placed, its point aimed toward one of the corners. If hung on a wall or placed atop a pole, the outside lines would be diagonal, and the crystal would point upward.

I constructed the cross from oak, with some leather at the corners and where the cross pieces met in the middle. My heart told me that the proper thing to do with this first cross was to give it to Jesus. The big rock that serves as nucleus of the medicine wheel, which probably averages about five feet in diameter, has a crevice beneath it that the cross could fit into. Maybe that's where I would put it, I thought. I drove to the farm with the cross on a summer afternoon that rapidly became cloudy. I walked up the mountain with thunder growling and the serious threat of a storm over my head. I didn't like that—I would normally never go out in a storm, especially to a mountaintop. However, I'd begun the gesture for Jesus, and turning back was unthinkable. To my wonderment, as soon as I arrived at the stone atop the mountain, the cloud drifted away, and sunlight poured through the leaves.

I climbed onto the rock and sat, the cross in my hands, my eyes closed.

I brought this to You, I thought. *Shall I put it on the stone or under the stone?*

Through my mind these words passed: *Gifts are given and received in the heart. You have given it. I have received it. Take it and keep it for Me.*

I went home with the cross.

When the ark was finished, it was pretty. Gleaming horizontal oak, walnut and maple boards alternated on its sides. At the center of each side, a one-inch hole was surrounded by dogwood strips in a diamond design. The top, covered in four triangular mirrors, rose to a point. Inside, the ark was lined with leather.

Our ark doesn't compete with the Ark of the Covenant, I'm sure, and it shouldn't. Obviously, we couldn't cover its surface with gold, but from what I've learned about ark-building, I'm convinced that the only importance of gold in the original ark was to have the Israelites' entire population participate in creating the ark by sacrificing a precious gift to its creation. In spiritual matters, the energy that we put into something is proportional to the energy that comes from it.

Following Ramoth's instructions, to go along with the ark we made four wooden staffs about five feet long. Each man made his own, with all three working together on William's. Just as the four wood species in the ark represented the four brothers, so did the staffs. Ken's was oak, John's walnut, William's maple, and mine dogwood. Each had a quartz crystal in one end, and each was wrapped with leather from the opposite end halfway up its length.

Each member of the star was to place a gift inside the box. My gift was the quartz cluster that I had spent a year moving from point to point around a big rock on my parents' farm. I also placed the new age cross in the box. It had been only a year since I wrote *Shakespeare's Latest Play* and even less time since the play's production on stage, and I was certain that Shakespeare had communicated to me that he wanted the play placed in the ark, so I laid a copy there. Each member of the star brought at least one gift to the ark. Those are personal matters, though, not for me to divulge.

Ramoth instructed us to wait until the next full moon, April 18, 2000. A few days before that, except for Leslie, who couldn't make it, we all got together at Ken's house. I'm sure we talked with Ramoth, but it's a different channeling that I remember vividly. Yvonne channeled Athor.

"Your light beams," said Athor. "It does not work by science, yet it beams, and I want it. You will give it to me."

We knew he meant the ark.

"Why should we give it to you?" asked John.

"You will have no choice. You cannot resist me. I am far more intelligent than you, and you fear me."

"I believe we disabled your craft," said Ken.

"Yes, and I destroyed it. It can be replaced," Athor said almost eagerly, as if the loss of a spaceship were equivalent to dropping a nickel onto the floor.

Somehow, Athor's talking to us had an effect opposite from his intentions. Instead of being intimidated, we all began to sense his weakness. I think of pride as an emotion, but maybe it can be as simple as a cold miscalculation. He assumed our stupidity and our fear of him. Not being a creature of God, he had no idea what he was really dealing with. Ken, John and I all sensed that he could be beaten. No doubt he meant to frighten us with a fact that we already knew, stating that his race's females had ceased reproducing, so he had ordered them destroyed.

Suddenly I had an inspiration, probably from Ramoth.

"If your females are dead, then who does your cooking?" I asked.

Ken and John chuckled.

"What? What? No." Athor was flustered. "We prepare our sustenance in a laboratory." (Mostly from seaweed, according to Ramoth.)

Athor prattled a bit more about his superiority and ended by assuring us that he would have the ark.

"What will you give us for it?" Ken asked slyly.

"No," said Athor. "You will give it to me."

"Come and get it," said Ken.

"Yes. I will have it."

"Because you're so intelligent," John grinned.

"Yes."

When Athor's energy left her, Yvonne wore a look of utter distaste and said she felt filthy inside and out.

I now believe that Athor's great weakness was his lack of emotion. In wisdom there's always an element of love. Without emotion there can be no wisdom, just intelligence—mathematics, if you will. Athor was unaware that we were teasing him. He was unaware that we were not afraid. He had no wisdom.

The eighteenth of April came, a fairly mild day but a damp one. By early evening, when we met at Ken's house, a drizzling fog swallowed all distance. We could see only a few hundred feet. Ramoth assured us that this was a big event, bigger than global. Pleiadeans would be watching. Angels would be present. Past lives would attend us. Ramoth had told John that the Grays might approach us on the ground. We all worried that something might go wrong, but it was a vague worry. We kept faith.

Quietly we moved the ark into Ken's back yard. John, Ken and I took up our staffs. Leslie held William's. Yvonne stood nearby. With Ramoth's help, she would direct our actions. Silently, somewhere above us Athor moved into position too. At Yvonne's command, John, Ken, Leslie and I stood facing the ark, each at one of the four sides. Then, together, we inserted the crystals at the ends of our staffs into the holes in the side of the ark and concentrated on sending God's white light through our bodies, into the staffs and on into the ark.

After only a few seconds, Yvonne said: "Athor is dead."

The battle for earth was won. And we were alive.

As we stepped away from the ark, we could all feel presences surrounding us. King Arthur and the knights were there. I smelled the horses and the leather. I felt an energy nearby and walked to it.

"Who is this?" I asked.

Ramoth answered through Yvonne: "Do you not recognize the Disciple?"

It was Jesus.

Later that night the five of us stopped at a quiet restaurant and shared a pizza.

The next time Yvonne held a Saturday-evening meeting, I walked into the room to find it abuzz with talk of the Grays' demise. Most people assumed that a tremendous military battle had taken place, but why had the media not reported it? Most of Yvonne's more faithful clients had had private readings earlier during the day, and some had heard the news then. One man, however, had consulted a different channel earlier in the week and already knew about it. The same man had once heard John say that he would someday fight the Grays.

"Were you involved in it?" he asked.

John shook his head. "No."

That man told the group that Ramoth and the other channel had said that non-military people had fought the aliens with the help of angels.

"By angels they must have meant Pleiadeans," he said. "It would take such advanced weapons to beat the Grays."

What he said sounds very reasonable, partly because we're all familiar with science fiction and partly because we human beings are a weapon-loving, warlike species. Frankly, I don't think the Pleiadeans have weapons, and aside from some sort of laser-like thing that caused guns to become so hot that people dropped them, I don't think the Grays had weapons either.

No, the Grays were done in by the same tool that made the walls of Jericho crumble—a box of divine will.

We didn't immediately kill all Grays when Athor died, somehow incinerated by intense light outside the visible spectrum. But within days they started dying because they couldn't live without him. Each Gray was a separate biological creature, but Athor was their brain, connected to them by mental telepathy, which science doesn't yet understand. Disconnected from the big brain, the Grays moved about aimlessly, not knowing what to do, not even knowing to feed themselves, apparently. Soon they were all dead.

Most of the world's more powerful governments knew about the Grays, certainly, and many of them probably got hold of alien hardware, whether or not they knew how to use it. Somebody must have gotten the craft that hovered in the sky not too far from Ken's house. Probably wisely, Ken left town for a few days. When he got back, Yvonne and I had placed 18 plastic pink flamingos in his back yard—18 because that's how many Wal-Mart had.

Ramoth told us that we would soon see something in the newspaper to validate our work on April 18. In less than a month there was news of a controlled burn that quickly became an out of control wildfire near Alamogordo, New Mexico. At the time I considered that a wildfire would be a plausible cover for destroying the bodies of dead Grays, and it would be, but the eventual news that four hundred homes were destroyed made me rethink that theory. I did soon see a small item in the local paper stating that the British UFO Society was disbanding because all alien activity appeared to have ceased.

In my own little sphere, I believe I saw increased productivity from students following the spring 2000 semester. It would be interesting to see if, nationally or internationally, grades, college board scores and other measurable facets of education showed an upswing beginning then.

When our star group formed, we were aware that there were eleven other such groups scattered across the planet. Each star group, Ramoth said, aside from a big project was also to work on a different problem. Ours was the relationship group. Leslie was the only member who had been able to maintain a marriage. The rest of us were divorced, some of us several times over. As a group, we maintained a good relationship as long as we had a collective purpose, but after the trip to England and several more uses of the ark, aside from Yvonne and me, the star members gradually drifted in different directions, although we're all still friends. In 2002, Yvonne and I were married and for a number of years thrived in our relationship, but unfortunately, in 2023 we separated. Aliens we can master, but in relationships, as a group we're still only so-so.

At one of our early star meetings, John joked that the courage group hadn't yet held a meeting. I hope, if there was a courage group, they did meet, but we never knew what problems the other groups were to work on. Only recently did John learn from Ramoth that all twelve groups worked with us against the Grays at the same time on April 18, 2000. Even more recently I learned that there were twelve groups of Grays, each with its own leader, but that the other leaders were less sinister than Athor, who ultimately wanted to create a hybrid race and destroy the rest of us.

Twelve star groups, twelve tribes of Israel, twelve Apostles, twelve notes in the chromatic scale. It means something, but I don't know what. I have no doubt that the members of the eleven other groups have stories parallel to and just as complex as my own. In my wildest hope, Jesus will return in my lifetime and bring the twelve stars together. What stories we could share.

Thirteen

Facing Demons

Under Ramoth's direction we would use the ark a few more times. In 2000 there were various local groups of people drawn to the dark side of spirituality. At that time I had several students who were avowed Satanists and others whom I knew, with Ramoth's help, to be witches. Many people were emitting dark energy.

Ramoth referred to people like the star group as light workers. A light worker is the opposite of a person who practices black magic. Black magic comes from the dark; it comes from evil. Light work comes from God. A light worker wouldn't use the power of light to try to force someone to love him or do his bidding. The ark turned out to be a powerful generator of light. Once misused, I'm sure it would from that moment on be nothing more than a box.

Sorcerers, wizards, witches (when the word is used in this sense) and the like work at best with earth energies, which I know little about, and at worst with dark energy. If they work with dark energy, their purpose is selfish, and they simply don't worry about karma. To them, the here and now is all-important.

Ramoth informed us that a "large" group of dark practitioners planned to meet on the bank of a certain river on a certain evening and sacrifice a dog in order to open a large "door" to allow dark energy to pour through. What he described was Satanic. We were to use the ark to thwart those people.

We used the ark in the same manner we'd used it before. Ramoth allowed Yvonne to see mentally what happened. When the lead sorcerer chanted and was just about to thrust a knife into the shaved neck of the dog, we guided the crystals of our wands into the holes in the ark, visualizing God's light pouring into it.

Elsewhere, a great blinding light bathed the scene of the dark ritual, terrifying those assembled. The sorcerer cried that the wrong door had opened, and people fell to the ground. Yvonne heard a voice yelling that someone had suffered a heart attack. The dog ran free. A week or so later, Ramoth said that after that night, many of those people had decided that Satanism was not such a good thing, after all. Two of those present, he said, were young people I knew from the college.

We used the ark twice more against smaller Satanic groups, one time apparently saving a young woman from becoming a sexual sacrifice at the edge of a lake.

At about that time I had an interesting experience in one of my classes. A female student who always wore black and sat in the left rear corner of the classroom decided one day to steal my energy. As I lectured, she looked steadily at me, tapping her thumb and forefinger rapidly together. I suddenly felt woozy and weak. My energy was draining. I knew what was happening, and I knew who was doing it. From the way she dressed, it wasn't hard to tell who was the witch in the room. I quickly surrounded myself with light and shot a beam of it straight at her without even looking directly her way. Her fingers stopped moving. When I glanced at her, she looked a bit stunned. My strength came back.

A very few days later, a woman came to my office door. She was the girl's mother, she said, just dropping by. I noticed that she wore black, like her daughter. We chatted for a few minutes; then she said she had to be on her way. We each knew what the other was, and we each knew the other knew that. The girl never zapped me again.

Ramoth had directed us in using the ark to combat local Satanists. We never considered that we might be building up to something larger. However, Ramoth soon told us that we would assist in bringing down a much bigger foe, bigger than the aliens, perhaps.

God created man, but man created Satan, according to Ramoth. That is not to say that Satan is imaginary—far from it. Satan is a real entity on earth, and we should all hope that earth is as far as his influence stretches. Surely that would be better than having it permeate the universe.

Satan's name doesn't appear in the Old Testament. There is the tempter—the serpent—in the Garden of Eden, but the tempter is not identified as the devil, a demon or Satan. There is also "the adversary" mentioned in the Book of Job, which in some translations appears as "Satan" or "the satan," but those are later translations. I have occasionally heard people say that in the Old Testament the king of demons is referred to as Beelzebub (or Baalzebub). The only reference I find of him is in II Kings 1. There he is very clearly identified as the god of Ekron, a Philistine city. That hardly puts him on a par with Satan. "Beelzebub" is possibly the name the Ekronites used for their maker, just as English-speaking people use "God" and French-speakers use "Dieu." The other possibility is that it is the name of a minor deity who supposedly watched over their particular city, not very different from a patron saint. In II Kings God's issue appears to be with the king Ahaziah for showing no belief in Him, not with Beelzebub. Unfortunately, it seems to have taken the deaths of 102 men for God to make His point—but I don't know anything about the karma of those 102 men, so I'll refrain from speculating on why they had to die at that time.

Could mankind have created Satan and his demons? If the ill-fated inhabitants of a planet in the Zeta Reticuli could have created a biological, thinking, functioning race lacking spirits, could our ancestors have created a "race" of evil spirits without bodies? It wouldn't take technology to make it happen. It might take nothing more than greed. Greed is the first of the great sins and the parent of all the other sins.

Let's consider the Garden of Eden. Some people believe the Genesis narrative to be literally true. As a poet, I'm used to language that is not literally true in one sense but is profoundly true in another. I see Genesis as being profoundly true; I don't care whether it's literally true. The story behind the surface story is always where the greater truth lies. In Genesis, God gives Adam and Eve dominion over the Garden of Eden, saving for Himself only the fruit of one tree. That fruit is His. It's human nature to see that fruit as being more desirable, more valuable, more irresistible than the Garden's other fruits. Adam and Eve experience greed. They have more than enough fruit, but they can't have *that* fruit. So they *must* have that fruit. They *must* have that fruit. The author of Genesis (presumably Moses) calls the tempter a serpent. The serpent embodies greed. Adam and Eve succumb to the parent of all sins. Within one generation the sin of greed has spawned the sin of murder.

When Abel, the first murder victim, died, his soul left his body and had the opportunity to go to the light, which embodies God's love and ultimately life. We have no reason to think that it didn't accept that opportunity. Eventually Cain died, too—died with a guilty soul. If that soul went to the light, it would have to face God. Some sort of reprimand would surely await. So the soul of Cain chose not to go to the light. It remained in a dark space, fretting, then festering and finally furious at God—furious at God instead of itself because of immaturity. Not all immature people are evil, thank heaven, but all evil people are immature. The wise embody maturity. Consider the wise: can anyone imagine Jesus stealing His neighbor's chickens, Buddha robbing a convenience store, Mohammed snatching an old lady's purse? Would Gandhi commit fraud?

As time went on, more evil souls chose like Cain's to cling to the dark. Some chose differently, to go to the light. If punishment awaited, they would accept it. But over time an army of angry, guilty souls accumulated, hating God and wanting to lash out. They couldn't reach God, but maybe they could influence man and thereby hurt God indirectly. Along the way they developed some sort of hierarchy, or at least a leader. Perhaps they called him Satan.

Jesus identified Satan as "the ruler of this world." Indeed, there are people in this world not ruled by Satan. But what does Satan embody most of all? Greed. Doesn't the desire to have what is not ours motivate the whole world? Is it not the chief author of history? Why do we have nuclear weapons? Because Nazi Germany and Japan of the 1940s wanted what was not theirs and blithely killed whoever got in the way of their desires. Is that not greed? Because that sort of greed continues and can easily explode into war, billions of dollars must be devoted yearly to an arms race when that money could easily feed the world, much of which is starving. Greed. Satan.

Did Satan create greed? No, greed is a little flame in the human ego, but Satan is certainly happy to pour gasoline on it, and once a person allows him to do that, the feeling of heightened greed becomes addictive. As Ramoth says, man is absolutely capable of great sin on his own, without the help of Satan and any demons, but a by-product of our sin is an army of vengeful, destructive souls who would influence each of us and destroy the world in order to wreak revenge on their Maker, who eventually would have forgiven them all if they had only chosen to go to the light.

It stands to reason, if we consider it true that God is life, that Satan and all demons are mortal. If one cuts oneself off from God, from the source of life, one must eventually run out of life. In Romans 6:23 Paul makes the often quoted statement: "the wages of sin is death." To those of us who go to the light following a death experience, life continues indefinitely, but refusal to go to the light cuts one off from his higher self, which Ramoth often mentions, that portion of the soul that resides in eternity and that we can call upon. Shakespeare, for example, channeled poems and plays from his higher self, Ramoth told me. Satan can't reach his higher self. Demons can't. Just as the

Grays, for all their technical knowledge, were no match for five people with a box and four sticks, Satan isn't much, and his demons are less. *People* can defeat them. All people with souls have connections straight to God if they choose to use them. The devils don't have that. The only weapon they have against us is that most of us are terrified of them. We don't have to be. As Ramoth once said: "Satan has never killed a man. He can't." You and I are more awesome than he.

Yvonne and I once destroyed a demon—killed it. It happened before our marriage, when Yvonne had an apartment and I was living alone in the small house I once had. We had come to her apartment after an outing at a nearby town, and apparently a demon had followed us back. As we sat on the couch, Yvonne became aware of the demon's presence. She told me what was happening and asked that I do as she instructed. She then commanded the demon in the name of light and God to stand on a mat just inside the front door. Unable not to obey, the demon did as told. At Yvonne's instruction, I joined her in concentrating God's white light onto the demon, which destroyed the evil spirit in the same way God's light had destroyed Athor only a short while earlier.

On another occasion, Ramoth told me during a reading that a "negative entity," or demon, had gotten into my house. When I got home, I picked up my wand, walked into the living room and said aloud: "There is a negative being in this house."

Immediately, I felt a tingling sensation somewhat like static electricity all along the right side of my body. The demon was attacking me. I began spinning in the room, waving the wand in a full circle around me, commanding the demon in the name of light and God to be gone. It left.

Ramoth prepared us for a battle against Satan himself. The Disciple—Jesus—was to destroy Satan on a certain day some months ahead, and we five (along with other people, I assumed) were asked to help. Ramoth required that each of us construct a cross small enough to place within the ark. We were all to be careful, he cautioned, because while we were being protected, there is no protection against one's own foolishness, and any reckless behavior could open a door for Satan's influence. I suppose he mentioned this to each of us, but I recall him telling me in a private reading that Satan might appear to me in my home.

One night I woke to the hiss of heavy breathing next to me in bed, quite a disturbing sound. I quickly called upon Jesus and God's white light. The breathing ceased. I turned on a light, then went through the house, room by room, turning on lights and filling each room with God's white light, commanding negativity to be gone. Afterward, I turned out all lights, got back into bed and—strangely, I think—slept well for the rest of the night.

On the evening of the attack, we all placed our crosses in the ark, then used it just as we had earlier against the Grays. When we were done, Ramoth asked us to close our eyes and consider what we saw. I saw the dead Satan, a dull brownish gray like the top half of a typical shark, shaped like a dirigible and deflating.

"The demons will come seeking their master, and master will not respond," Ramoth said. Soon, though, they would select another master, and his name would be Satan also. Satan, he explained, is not so much a name as a title. Satan, like all other demons, eventually dies.

Recently I asked Ramoth if the destruction of Satan on that night in early 2001 happened simply to demonstrate demons' mortality to our star group and perhaps some other people. Such a demonstration was more a by-product, he said. That particular Satan would have done a great deal of damage had he been allowed to live. In the nuclear age, one shudders to think what that damage might have been. Jesus was looking out for us.

Demons are mortal; even Satan is mortal. If we human beings all lived in the light of God and practiced enough charity to offset our greed, in death we would all happily enter God's light, and in time all demons would expire of something like old age, never to bother us again.

I hope that can happen, but it will require changing a pattern. We'll all need to become students of life and not its victims. We'll need to temper our envy of those with wealth, fame and power. Do we not realize that those people fall prey to alcohol, drugs and suicide the same as the poor? No, the lives and souls of the "beautiful" people can seldom hold a candle to the simpler lives and souls of the happy people. We need to emulate the wise. The tendency to feel greed is indeed a part of the human ego. We need to realize that and make a conscious effort to aim our attention toward the love of God and not at His golden apple. Only then will we break the cycle.

Fourteen

Prepping for the Coming Age

My spiritual journey—the part of it that distinguishes it from the typical person's spiritual journey in my day—began when I learned that I, a virtually unknown living poet who wrote only sporadically—was the reincarnation of a major poet of the relatively recent past. Such a revelation seems unbelievable to the average person until it happens to that average person. In just a generation or two, though, I think knowing something about one's past lives will be the rule, not the exception. It's already more commonplace than some people realize. I know dozens of people who are aware of at least some past lives, but they don't write books about it and don't tell anyone except their most trusted confidants.

A session with a hypnotherapist who is open to past-life work is one way to start exploring past lives. Knowing the past often helps us understand the present. In fact, just knowing who I had once been allowed many things in my life to make sense. I got a better handle on relationship issues I'd faced. I understood why I liked what I liked, why I had studied what I did, why I was who I was. Anyone could benefit from that. As Jesus said: "Know thyself."

That some of my past lives had involved being relatively well-known people didn't swell my ego. It could do that to some people, but likely wouldn't. Glory ends on the death bed. I know several people who have had historically significant lives, but in every case they're not intrigued so much by the fame of those lives as by the struggles of those lives—struggles just like those that everyone faces. It's who we are today that matters, but part of knowing who we are should be knowing who we were. It brings a wealth of understanding and allows us to retire karma more efficiently. Besides that, it's self-exploration. It's fun. And at this point in time, it's what God wants us to do.

Jesus will soon be among us again. When He came before, He wasn't what most people expected, and religious leaders were in the forefront in denouncing Him. When He stands among us, once again He won't be what most people expect, and religious leaders once again will seek to discredit Him. He might come as a Jew; He did before. The likelihood that He comes as a Christian is probably small. What will the evangelists have to say about that?

When He comes, it will be to lead us out of the hell we've created for ourselves. He will rebuke our leaders, both political and religious. He will rebuke the greedy and the ostentatious. He will be unimpressed by those who expect to impress Him. Remember, He will be a lion, not a lamb. He will be a protector, not a sacrifice. He *is* the Son of God. But many people will not believe that.

The spiritual will hear Him, will want to follow Him. He will be here to lead humanity onto a higher plane. He will bring the great truths of the world's religions together. He will speak of God, karma and reincarnation all in the same sentence. He will open people's minds to their own past lives and show them the way to better future lives. He will still be the way—that is, the traveler and the path—and we will have the opportunity to follow Him toward God. We will also have the option to call Him a fraud and dismiss Him. It happened before.

Yvonne, Leslie, Ken, John and I were privileged to enter the New Age a few years ahead of the majority of people. Not one of us knows why. Yvonne is the most blessed of us, chosen to channel the words and energy of Ramoth, God's servant. I'm blessed, chosen to write this book—blessed despite the certainty that it will bring me ridicule and censure in the short term and probably distance me from friends and relatives for the rest of my life.

In writing the book, I have prayed every day that God would not allow me to make any mistake in wording or memory that would distort the truth. I've asked Ramoth if I have misrepresented anything, and he has said that I have not. As I stated at the beginning, I'm willing to submit to a polygraph test, hypnosis or any other reasonable procedure to verify the truth of any and all contents of this book. I'm sure that my fellow star members feel the same.

I recently asked Ramoth about the other eleven star groups. I had thought that maybe Ramoth led them all, but he said that each of them was led by a different guide. The separate groups were scattered across the globe, had different religious backgrounds, were given different assignments and all served God and mankind. Only our star group built and used an ark, but every group created something. Not all groups were able to meet their goals, and some individuals suffered emotional distress as a result. I'm sorry for that and feel for those disappointed individuals.

I recall Ramoth saying some years back that a star group was located in the vicinity of Stonehenge, another at the Egyptian pyramids and one in Cambodia. Recently he told me that with the information I had about the four (including my own), I could find the others. Using a borrowed globe and a compass—not the magnetic kind but the kind we draw circles with—I went to work. There was a great distance between Roanoke and Stonehenge and a great distance between the pyramids and Cambodia, so I adjusted the legs of the compass to the straight line distance between Stonehenge and the pyramids. Then I set one leg of the compass on Roanoke and let the other leg pass over North America, discovering that it passed right across Sedona, Arizona, a high-energy location where many ley lines are said to cross. From Sedona the compass found the south coast of Mexico's Yucatan Peninsula, also believed to be a high-energy spot. From there the compass led me across South

America, where the most likely looking spot was along the border between Ecuador and Peru.

Then I set the compass on Cambodia and saw that it reached Nepal. How could there not be a star group in Nepal? From Nepal the compass could reach the pyramids if it made a stop in Oman. Between Egypt and Oman I found a spot in Kenya. Also, from Egypt the compass reached an area slightly east of Moscow, from there it reached the Russian city Novosibirsk, and from that location it reached back to Nepal. Triangulating from Nepal and Cambodia, I found an area in China just west of Beijing.

In all, I'd found 13 possible locations for the 12 star groups. Of the 13, 11 were correct, but I'd actually found the locations of all 12 groups because Sedona had two groups, according to Ramoth. I also discovered from Ramoth that not all groups had five members, as ours did. A total of 32 people filled the two groups in Sedona. The South American group was also large, made up of people from both Ecuador and Peru. The star group in Kenya had 12 members, the Nepalese group had eight members, and the Russian groups were both large. As it turns out, I was wrong in believing there might have been groups in Oman and China.

It's usually more satisfying to discover something than to be told it, and I appreciate that Ramoth gave me just enough information to solve a puzzle. He is, among other things, a very skillful teacher—better than I ever was.

I know little about ley lines, but I know that some sort of earth energy grid criss-crosses the planet. Obviously, all of the star groups were located on important points on that grid, and the distance between Stonehenge and the pyramids connects all of them, although there is an apparent disconnect between the sites in the Europe-Africa-Asia area and those in the Americas. I can offer no explanation, just a pattern, but there are plenty of knowledgeable people in the world who can explain it. I want them to, and I want to see or hear the explanation.

Fifteen

God, Man, Religion, Science

I was 22 when I experienced my first waking past-life memory. I was in my dorm room at the University of North Carolina at Greensboro practicing Transcendental Meditation, which simply calls for a person to sit quietly with eyes closed, repeating a mantra for 20 minutes. Sometimes, one falls asleep. Other times, one lapses into a lazy mental state and forgets to repeat the mantra. It's just like any other meditation except that I had paid money to learn to do it. It was money well spent, though, because previously I didn't know how to meditate. As for the mantra, I suspect that I could just as well have repeated the name of my dormitory building or any other word. It's the calming repetition and the simple focus on the word that allows one to slip into the meditative state.

I had apparently slipped into that state when in my mind I saw my feet as if I were standing, looking down. I wasn't wearing shoes, exactly. Around each foot was a piece of leather pulled up around the ankle and held there by a leather strip tied in a knot. I looked up and outward from my feet and first saw the hooves, then the front legs of horses and finally the men sitting astride them. These men were medieval knights, finely dressed, helmeted, humorless. I had the distinct feeling that I was in trouble. At that point the vision ended, and I came out of the meditation.

Over 20 years passed before I asked Ramoth about the experience. He verified that it was a past-life memory.

"You were near where France and Italy join now," he said.

"Was I in trouble?"

"Yes. You were very hungry and had taken an apple from a tree in an orchard."

"What was the outcome?"

"Your death."

Let's hope the laws in that area are a bit more lenient today. Nevertheless, the story illustrates a moral complexity that has always been part of human life. To kill a man over an apple is extreme, yet to do nothing about the theft of the apple could be to invite every peasant for miles around to come and gather fruit. That would be an invasion possibly resulting in the loss of an entire apple crop that the owner of the orchard and his serfs and knights depended on.

"I'm starving, and you have countless apples," I might have said.

"You're a thief, and to keep more thievery from occurring, we must make an example of you," the knights might have said. Or they might have dispensed with words altogether. After all, they *were* there to kill me.

After becoming a student of Ramoth, I adopted the simple moral code of always choosing the light. Another way of saying that is to ask *What would Jesus do?* and let the answer direct my choice. Yet there are difficult situations, gray areas like the one above, vexing conundrums that require reasoned, wise thought and make us wiser through solving them. *What would Jesus do?*

Today, as I write this, in various parts of the world emigrants and refugees amass at borders or pass illegally across them in numbers that really do resemble invasions. One person fleeing hardship is pitiful and worthy of charity, but what can be done when thousands upon thousands of such people arrive, all needing help?

Morality's gray areas have always been complex, but they involve larger numbers of people than ever before, and they cross national boundaries, religious boundaries, political boundaries and economic boundaries. They are not the problems of this group or that group. They are mankind's problems, and as such, in order to solve them, peoples—not people—need to come together. We need for the greatest minds in spirituality, science, economics, politics and religion to find common ground—if they possibly can—to think in new ways, to break old cycles and to find ways to meet the needs of our fellow human beings. Would anything please God more?

Is anything less likely? The scientific community generally disdains the spiritual community. The religious community generally demonizes both the spiritual and the scientific communities. Politicians often use the ideas of economists, but that volatile mixture led to Stalin's Russia and, partially in reaction to that, Hitler's Germany. Yet clearly these groups must come together if human beings—our children and their children (our own reincarnations)—are to survive.

It is inevitable that the new age, probably born of global war plus the Second Coming, will spawn a great interconnectedness of diverse groups and diverse thought.

Science and spirituality will eventually merge, inevitably. Nowadays many religious people are *taught* to believe that the two are antithetical, that science is totally atheistic. Yet Albert Einstein believed in God, and many other scientists do as well—but some of them don't necessarily believe in God in a religious sense. (God's existence does not depend on religion.) Science seeks to discover how the universe works. Religion seeks to worship the creator of the universe. Let's draw a picture.

Get a sheet of paper, or if you have a vivid imagination, envision a sheet of paper. Draw a horizontal line across the paper from left to right. At the right end of the line, draw a sideways V so as to make an arrow of the line. At the left end of the line, write the word "God." We've now drawn a graph of Creation in that we have God and an arrow indicating all things coming from Him. God had to make the universe and earth before He could put us on earth, correct? So just to the right of the word "God," write the word "earth," and to the right of that, write "man." The arrow is now both a graph of Creation and a timeline. The earth came first, then man.

Man, with the gift of free will, has been allowed to create many things, apparently without much interference from God. Artillery, machineguns, intercontinental ballistic missiles and atomic bombs are just a few examples. Who made religion, God or man? If God made religion, then why are there so blasted many of them on the face of the earth? Did God cause people to worship Beelzebub? Did God cause people to worship Zeus? Of course not. So write the word "religion" on the horizontal line to the right of the word "man." Also, above that horizontal line, draw another line, this one pointing from man to religion. Man created religion to help him explain, and worship, the greatest mystery in the universe, its Creator. If man created religion, then surely man created science, but science came later, so write "science" on the horizontal line to the right of "religion." To complete the graph, draw a looping line from "man" to his creation "science," but don't draw it through the word "religion."

The purpose of this graph isn't to negate religion but simply to show that religion and science are both creations of man and that both spring from the same human impulse—to honor truth. If people sincerely honor God, they will honor any path that leads to Him. If they are convinced of God's existence, they should have faith that any inquiry into the workings of the universe cannot fail to bring us closer to His truth and thus to Him. Or do they value religion more than they value God?

If so, these are the very people who won't know Jesus when He stands before them. "Oh, no," they'll say. "I know who the Savior is, and it's not you!" That's been said before, some two thousand years ago. The time has come for believers to learn from that mistake.

Now, if religion and science are man-made—but both useful—and spirituality is a God-given human trait as well as the *basis* of religion (Adam and Eve talked with God, and Old Testament people talked with God and angels, and such interaction is spiritual and occurs even today), then spirituality should be recognized as infusing all human endeavors. If mankind is to be functional instead of grossly dysfunctional, then spirituality must be a part of science, religion, economics and politics.

It is the lack of spirituality that makes science, religion, economics and politics deadly.

Dog-ear this page and underline the previous sentence. It bears being thought about.

So-called common sense, which many people use effectively on a daily basis, seems to hold little sway when applied to large groups—nations, for instance. Huge groups seem to revert to basic, immature instincts: *I want, so I must have; I'm important, but you're not.*

Recently I recalled Ramoth speaking about the common sense behind the Ten Commandments at one of Yvonne's group meetings. I asked him to repeat his thoughts on the subject. It is worth noting, he told me, that when Moses came down the mountain with the Ten Commandments, he was presenting them to very backward people who essentially had no moral compass. Wanting something easily led to theft. Self-centeredness easily led to murder. For such people, the Ten Commandments had to be simply stated. While they are just as valid today as they were then, some of them don't cover the gray areas well. At the time, they couldn't. "They should be thought of in the historical context," Raymoth said. I'll quote the Ten Commandments from the King James Bible. The comments beneath each commandment paraphrase or summarize Ramoth's thoughts.

Thou shalt have no other gods before me.

At the time of Moses this referred more to the gods of the Egyptians and other peoples, yet in modern times it should be taken to refer to those things some people would give their souls for, such as money, prestige and power.

Thou shalt not make unto thee any graven image, or any likeness of any thing that is in heaven above, or that is in the earth beneath, or that is in the water under the earth.
People of Moses's time had trouble distinguishing between a symbol and what it symbolized. Thus, if they made a golden idol, they worshipped the molded gold rather than whatever it was meant to represent. Although on the surface this commandment appears to make serious sinners of children who draw pictures of trees and adults who paint or sculpt, Ramoth says that it really is meant to keep us from creating for ourselves false impressions of what God, Jesus or angels look like. He explained that it is impossible for an artist to create an accurate image of God because no artist knows what God looks like. The same is true with Jesus. If we are used to seeing pictures of Jesus with white skin and brown hair, will we recognize Him if He appears racially different? As for angels, Ramoth said that while angels are beautifully wonderful, not all are physically beautiful. We're better off not to associate heavenly beings with preconceived images.

Thou shalt not take the name of the Lord thy God in vain: for the Lord will not hold him guiltless that taketh his name in vain.
This has always meant to speak only with respect of and to God, and now the same is true in regard to Jesus.

Remember the Sabbath day, to keep it holy.
It is important to have a day of reflection each week, Ramoth said, although it does not matter which day.

Honor thy father and thy mother: that thy days may be long upon the land which the Lord thy God giveth thee.

Again, in Moses's time the concept of gratitude was not universally known. Parents care for their small children. When the children become adults and their parents falter physically, who will care for them? Surely people should respect their parents, but the original intent of this commandment was to provide for the elderly and to keep families cohesive.

Thou shalt not kill.
This is self-explanatory, yet Ramoth pointed out that there are instances in which one must kill, as in war or when a righteous person must kill to defend his own life or others' lives. The prohibition is against predatory killing.

Thou shalt not commit adultery.
Obviously, adultery can lead to a host of problems and is wisely avoided, but the greatest problem at the time of Moses was rape. Lacking a moral compass, men thought little of raping others' wives, and young girls at puberty were frequently victimized. Today we tend to think of adultery as consensual and of rape as a separate issue, one that thou still shalt not do.

Thou shalt not steal.
Self-explanatory, said Ramoth.

Thou shalt not bear false witness against thy neighbor.
Although this appears to refer to a particular type of lie, Ramoth said, it actually includes all lying.

Thou shalt not covet thy neighbor's house, thou shalt not covet thy neighbor's wife, nor his manservant, nor his maidservant, nor his ox, nor his ass, nor any thing that is thy neighbor's.
This is a very specific list of things that should not be coveted, so specific because of the limited understanding of the stiff-necked people under Moses's charge. The commandment refers

to all things covetable, far greater in number today than in ancient times. Ramoth pointed out that to covet is essentially to contemplate theft. Coveting is a sin that can lead to any of a number of other sins and is highly akin to greed.

The Ten Commandments represent tremendous wisdom, maybe the greatest wisdom the ancient world has to offer. However, the strong word "commandment" rankles some people. If those people preferred to think of them as the "Ten Highly Logical Recommendations," and if that helped those people accept them, wouldn't that be better than a refusal to contemplate them altogether? A lifetime spent working with the English language has taught me that if something can be said one way, it can be said a hundred ways. Being so caught up in wording that one cannot see the intent of a statement is akin to self-inflicted blindness. People who cannot distinguish a word from the meaning behind the word are like those ancient Israelites dancing around a golden calf who so infuriated their leader, Moses.

The value in the Ten Commandments is the wisdom contained in them, the moral compass that, collectively, they present to a world that has never completely accepted a moral compass. But we are close to the point where only a clear moral direction can save us. Semantics is far too petty a thing for us to argue over when billions of lives are at stake. Still, it's worth noting that while most of the people who would read this book live more or less within the moral sphere outlined by the commandments, many of the world's most powerful individuals and their cronies—the people who make the global decisions—do not.

One of the greatest problems between religion and science is a matter of semantics. Most of the problem lies in Chapter 1 of Genesis, which presents the account of Creation. Let's look at the Bible's first chapter as if we're seeing it for the first time and consider what it might really refer to, knowing what we know today.

Day 1

God creates light and divides it from darkness

Ramoth has always referred to "God's white light" as something separate from the light of the sun and the stars. He encourages us to surround ourselves in it. When I once asked him what I could do to help Jesus, he suggested that when praying I send Him white light to help Him in His work. It was God's white light that we channeled in destroying the Gray leader. This light is beyond the visible spectrum but is clearly powerful. Surely the light of God was His first creation.

Day 2

God creates a firmament that divides waters above from waters below and calls the firmament heaven

In the dictionary, the firmament is defined as a hemispherical dome that covers the (apparently flat) earth and supports the stars, moon and sun. Typically, people say that "firmament" refers to "sky," but what if we see it as meaning "space"? God creates space and in it, distantly separated planets (above and below earth and including earth) that contain water, which we believe is essential for any life. Now we have something: God creates the universe.

Day 3

God divides land and water on earth and brings forth plants

This is a very simplistic statement, but it is consistent with science. Plants definitely came before animals.

Day 4

God creates stars, the moon and the sun

Clearly, steps 3 and 4 are reversed. The stars, the moon and the sun must be in place before there can be plants. Imagine the temperature on earth if the sun weren't in the sky.

Day 5

God creates fowls and water creatures, including whales

Science believes that the first mammals appeared around 200 million years ago and the first birds appeared 50 million years later. However, Genesis uses the word "fowls" possibly because there was yet no word for the first feathered creature—the dinosaur. Paleontologists have recently discovered that many dinosaur species were covered with feathers, and it has been known for some time that a few of them even flew. Science also believes that whales evolved from mammals similar to the hippopotamus, but at the same time that feathered dinosaurs roamed the land, whale-like dinosaurs swam the sea. The events of Day 5 refer to dinosaurs.

Day 6

God creates animals and man

If we accept the existence of God, there is nothing to argue about here.

My interpretation of the first chapter of Genesis, to which Ramoth has given his stamp of approval, is based on two simple concepts. The first is that although we might use the best word we have to describe something, that word still might be imperfect in clearly conveying the true intended meaning. The second is that God Himself did not write the Bible; He gave visions and information to human beings who did their very best to convert those visions and information to words. If you had never heard of a dinosaur and God showed you a picture of a feathered animal and a big beast in the water, what could you call those animals other than fowl and whale? And if God gave you a list of six items, all of which seemed abstract to you, is it not possible that you could accidentally reverse the order of items 3 and 4? And now for the big one: If you were a writer in very primitive times, with a primitive vocabulary, and you were shown that something occurred in six stages, is it likely that you had a good word for "stage," meaning a step in a process? Would "day" not be a logical word to use? Besides, a day—a rotation of the planet—cannot exist before the sun is in the sky and the earth is formed in proximity to it (Genesis refers to days *before the sun is placed in the sky*). Furthermore, a day on earth is different from a day on Mars, which is different from a day on Venus, and all of those are different from a day on Mercury. Who could possibly know what a day is to God?

The six days become the eons. God makes something, tinkers with it, makes it better, makes it more complex, takes His time with it because He has eternity to fill, and as science looks at the evidence of what God has done, it sees a continuing process. It sees evolution. It sees Creation. And God isn't finished. If He were, what would He do with the rest of eternity?

What I see on the first two pages of the Bible is something like a time capsule devised by God and meant to be opened in the twenty-first century. Until very recently the account of Creation read like a myth that must be accepted on faith by folks who had less knowledge than we, but now, thanks to science, we have the key to understanding on an entirely different level what God revealed, presumably to Moses, a long time ago.

Genesis and science are not at odds. But some religious leaders and their trusting followers choose to be at odds with science. Once again, those are the folks who won't know Jesus when He knocks at their door.

God is eternal, and the search for God is an eternal quest. Those who think they have all the answers are not only wrong and stagnating, but they are missing out on life's greatest offering—the search and the discoveries made within it. Discovery is the essence of learning and the wonder of life. It's a gift from God.

Sixteen

Path to the Future

The nature of written biographies is soon to change. As gaining access to information about past lives becomes more acceptable, every biography can be written anew. Not only will writers look into their subjects' lives but also into their past lives and even, in the case of those dead a while, into their future lives. Imagine—just when you hope everything has been written about William Butler Yeats, some newfangled type of biographer comes up with a book that links the lives of Yeats, Keats, the Pearl Poet, Gawain, Petrarch, Thomas Wyatt the Elder, the soldier Monroe Bradley and even myself. Something much like a new kind of genealogy is on its way. (There's a really intriguing connection between Wyatt and Petrarch; any encyclopedia-level discussion of Wyatt will probably reveal it.)

The Woman, obviously, links Keats, Yeats and me, but she was also lurking around in Camelot. Both of my ex-wives and at least one of my early girlfriends were also in Yeats's life. Yeats's parents reincarnated as my parents. Both Yeats and I had a red pony (known as a "sorrel" to a master of horses). During my teaching career, I had two co-workers who were previously uncles to Yeats. I met the poet Stephen Spender, who as a young man met Yeats. I've taught reincarnations of Ezra Pound and W.H. Auden, two poets who knew Yeats. I was taught by the reincarnation of John Millington Synge, a playwright well known to Yeats (and the reincarnation of Charles Dickens). In my present life, I've known reincarnations of all of Yeats's siblings. The list goes on.

Consider the New Age biographies of other writers. Francis Scott Fitzgerald had been Francis Scott Key and, at the time of Shakespeare, the London playwright Thomas Decker. The

Medieval poet Geoffrey Chaucer became, in succession, poets Edmund Spenser, John Milton, Percy Bysshe Shelley and T.S. Eliot. William Blake became Walt Whitman. Colonial American poet Anne Bradstreet became Emily Dickinson. Edgar Allan Poe became Robert Louis Stevenson, who became H.P. Lovecraft, who is writing under yet another name today. To prove that God has a sense of humor, poet Robert Burns became Robert Frost.

In United States history, Harry S. Truman had been Ulysses S. Grant, Francis D. Roosevelt had been George Washington, Theodore Roosevelt had been Andrew Jackson, and Abraham Lincoln, by way of a walk-in, had been Thomas Jefferson. Fittingly, Martin Luther King, Jr., had been Frederick Douglass. Elvis Presley had been Rudolph Valentino. Thomas Edison had been Benjamin Franklin. With the exception of the occasional new soul entering the mix, everyone was someone—in fact, many someones, many fascinating stories.

In the U.K., Prime Minister Winston Churchill had been the nineteenth-century Prime Minister Benjamin Disraeli. To my surprise, Ramoth said, Disraeli was the first incarnation of that particular soul. Field Marshall Bernard Montgomery had been Arthur Wellesley, the 1st Duke of Wellington, who defeated Napoleon. I suggest you consider his first name. Richard the Lionhearted became Richard II, who became Henry VII, and had once been Mordred. William III, also known as William of Orange, became—hold your hat—Wild Bill Hickok.

Ramoth says that something in our genes connects us to our past lives and that the necessary technology to make that connection already exists. That doesn't mean that scientists *recognize* that the technology exists or know exactly what to look for. Why would they have even thought about it? I hope someone will start thinking about it, though. I'm ready to offer my DNA, and Yeats has descendants who maybe might conceivably offer some of their own. After all, Yeats *did* believe in reincarnation and *was* a New Age thinker. To prove that he came back, even as me, would be a fine vindication for him. And I'd love to meet those descendants.

Also, a lock of Keats's red hair is on display at the Keats-Shelley Memorial House in Rome (both Keats and Shelley died in Italy). If any DNA could be salvaged from that, it might provide a further connection to Yeats's and mine.

I've often wondered what it would be like to spend time with Keats and Yeats. I certainly hope to do it on the other side and believe it will happen. After all, Ramoth says, everything I write gets critiqued endlessly (eternally, even?) by the two of them. They still write, he adds, but their new poetry is "a tad more celestial" than what they left for us to read. Perhaps when I get to the other side, the three of us will critique the verse of the poor schmuck I reincarnate into. I might even get to write some celestial verse.

It's strange to know that my soul lived the lives of Keats and Yeats, that it poured onto paper the poems they wrote. As a poet myself, I don't believe that anything I've written is comparable to the best works of either of them, and I know that in this life I haven't worked as hard as they did to write poetry. Even before I knew of my connection to them, however, I was influenced by them both, consciously drawing from their techniques and fully believing they were the masters I wanted to follow. I learned imagery and objectivity from Keats; whether that would be apparent to an educated reader, I don't know. I learned poetic sentencing from Yeats—the withholding of key words until close to the end of a sentence so as to build to a climax. I have had people tell me that doing so is old-fashioned and therefore in error, but I do it, and it's on display in "Confession," the poem about the Pearl Poet that I included in Chapter 6.

I've accomplished two things in verse that I believe both Keats and Yeats would applaud. They would see *Shakespeare's Latest Play*, even if I did channel it, as something worth the read. They would also like that I invented a form of poetry unique to myself. In the 1990s, before I knew of my past lives, I developed what I call logometric poetry. Logometrics measures lines by the number of words they contain. Again I'll refer to "Confession," which has four words in each line. Most of my logometric poems have been in stricter forms than "Confession," however. My first logometric poem, "A Fine Address," was in a form I call a "fiver," and I've written dozens of fivers. They're unrhymed and feature five stanzas of five lines each, with each line containing five words. Thus, every fiver is exactly 125 words long. I also devised a form I call a "sixxet." Based loosely on a sonnet, a sixxet has 14 unrhymed lines of six words each and is split into two stanzas of six lines followed by a two-line stanza—84 words in all. I placed a sixxet, "Nature's Circles," in Chapter 12. Below are two fivers, the first one ever and one I wrote in fall 2023.

A Fine Address

Something is scaling the foundations,
tracking minutely up white walls,
prying under latched window screens,
dropping unnoticed into clean kitchens
of houses in happy suburbia.
Suburban houses are gathering age
slowly, a paint blister here,
there a dented garage door,
a closet light not working
in little sister's pastel room.

Second Smile

So long ago I knew
a girl whose lovely face
resolved itself around a scar
above her eye, a mark
as perfect as the face
it made complete. And once
another girl lifted her blouse,
bitterly, for me to see
the raised line she hated
though it had saved her

The little sisters of suburbia,
who say their nightly prayers
and sleep with fluffy dogs
that never tasted blood, believe
pre-packaged lives wait on shelves
like fat-free snacks aerobic mothers
munch in cheerful kitchen nooks.
In dark closets of suburbia,
gathering strength, the future broods
like teenage thugs; even now
something is scaling the foundations,
seeking the high kitchen shelves
of carefree suburbia, bringing in
the great beyond, the untamed
all this neighborhood fenced out.

from cancer and early death.
How often the body's scars
become the soul's, dark truths
to hide like shameful acts.
But let me this morning
raise an old man's mug
of coffee to that girl
whose face I still recall
for beauty made more precious
by a kiss of happenstance,
the artistry of life itself
that makes the broken new,
the second smile of one
who suffered once yet bore
her mending with sweet grace.

Using fivers, I wrote a suite of poems that Yeats would probably like but that Keats might not relate to. On my drive home from teaching one day, a fiver started coming to me. Concerned that I would forget it otherwise, I pulled into a parking lot to jot it down. That began a project that filled my spare time for the next 21 days. The first fiver in the suite was "The Fool," which refers to the first card in that part of the Tarot deck that's called the Major Arcana. I knew a little about the Tarot, enough to be familiar with the cards, but I've certainly never been an expert on the subject, nor have I ever been able to use the Tarot for any psychic purpose. However, averaging one poem per day, I produced 22 fivers, each one "expressing" its corresponding card. The fiver was a perfect form for those poems because it made all of them exactly alike in format and even in word length. A few months later I found myself writing a prose paragraph to accompany each poem. Frankly, I like the poems very much and knew just enough about Tarot to have written them, but the prose explanations are, to me, the most mystical part of the project. I didn't know I was going to write them until the moment I started, and while that's also true of the first poem in the sequence, I simply have never known enough about the Tarot to have written those explanations. Once I had completed them all, I was astonished at how insightfully they referred to one another. I must have channeled them.

As an example of the poems and their explanations, below is the poem I wrote for Card 13, *Death,* and the prose passage that accompanies it (in italics) with names of other Major Arcana cards capitalized:

Card 13

Death

As surely as day's end,
in chrysalid shroud I come,
my hook playing no favorites,
my eyes empty and deep.
My shadow reaches even you.

Fear of change and pain
of loss am I, but
joy of gain you wouldn't

dare predict I also am.
So shudder, flowers; cower, strength;

hide in rouge and wardrobe,
autumn grace. Forget what brought
the hyacinths. My bones creak
like an old, familiar wheel
as you flail the current

of a stream whose name
already you forget. Dust to
dust, you mutter. God to
God, my harvest mimes. See
how you work the fields

and fail the lesson offered
year by year—from living
stalk to grain, from grain
to flour, from flour to
bread, from bread to life.

If we shiver at ***Death*** *(Card 13), our shiver is the work of the ego, not of the life force within us. Indeed, the Death card is really an indication of continuing, growing life—a card of birth. In the Major Arcana, Death is merely the natural and proper movement from one state to another. While life can never truly be extinguished, today's ego can—and should—be replaced by tomorrow's better, wiser ego. Therefore, in his willing sacrifice of personal aspects that serve him poorly, the Hanged Man transitions from his former, weaker self to his new, stronger self. Any meaningful movement around the rim of the Wheel of Fortune involves such a transition. Death, then, is change, evolution, progress—from child to adult, from neophyte to master, from seed to seedling to sapling to towering tree. Death represents nothing more than mileposts on the path of Justice, the path of growth.*

It is movement, and it need not be abrupt and harrowing, for its effects are both created and offset by Temperance. Key: Transformation

Collectively, I call the Tarot poems *Major Arcana*. Yeats would like them, no doubt. He loved Tarot, astrology and things of that nature. He would certainly approve of the last quarter-century of my life, my studies and discoveries under Ramoth and the efforts that my friends and I made to help the unseen guardians of this world. A week ago today, just after I had written something about him, I think Yeats gave me a little poem. It flooded into my head so fast that I had to scurry to find paper before I forgot it. It isn't an important poem, just a rhyme, but it sounds like something that would fit into his collected works. Here it is, with a title that I added:

The Old Man in the Park, to His Shadow

I have loved women, and some have loved me;
some flew away, and some I set free.
The seasons now bend me; my path is now slow.
Where love went to winter, I never shall know.

Good one or bad one, I'm a poet. It's in my soul; it's what I was born to be. If I hadn't been a poet, one Saturday in 1997 I couldn't have known to ask Ramoth the one question that opened the door to so many questions, so many answers: *Were we in Ireland?* I've published only a few of my poems, mostly in little magazines that no one reads. For decades I've told anyone who cared to ask that I write first for God, second for the dead poets and third for any living person who might happen to read something I wrote. Maybe I was never meant to publish, never meant to develop even a little following or a little reputation. Anyone with a following or a reputation to lose could hardly afford to write a book like this one. No, I think I followed the poet's path just as I was meant to, eventually to that humble little room above a bookstore, where I asked a life-altering question. If I'm right about that, maybe in God's eyes I'm a good and somewhat obedient poet. I'd take that over a Nobel Prize any day.

I'd like to leave you with a few words first of caution and later of encouragement. In I John 2: 18 the Apostle writes: "As ye have heard that antichrist will come, even now are there many antichrists." The antichrists that he speaks of are demons, which once were the souls of men and women and now are doomed to defy God through deceiving us—and ultimately are also doomed to die because they have cut themselves off from God's life-sustaining energy. These demons can attach themselves to people and try to influence them, sometimes successfully. In more extreme cases, they can get into people and possess them. Surround yourself with God's white light frequently, and always demand in the name of God and light that all negativity leave you alone.

Also be aware that, according to Ramoth, there are living people who have no souls. The conscience is the voice of the soul, and where there is no conscience at all, there is no soul. Some people are born without souls, especially at this point in history when there are more births happening than there are souls needing to incarnate. In other cases, people willingly give up their souls because they simply don't want to be bothered by their consciences. People devoid of souls are very likely to take on demons. The demons offer power, and the soulless want it. Psychology has names for these individuals.

We hear people dreading the arrival of the Antichrist. I wish there were only one Antichrist and that his time were far in the future. But there have been numerous Antichrists, more than one in the twentieth century and more than one today. These are individuals who have either sent away or never had souls and who have allowed into their bodies the greatest and fiercest of demons—the kind of demon who might be in line to become the next Satan. They might talk about love, but they don't care about love and have none to give. They want power, and they want to be known. Study the history of the last century or so, and learn from it. And remember that words frequently lie, but actions seldom do.

Now for some encouragement. I invite you to join the quest I've been on for nearly three decades. In the early days I tried palm readers, Tarot readers, an astrologer and a few general psychics, who I believe were empaths. For me, the channel Yvonne was the answer because she put me in touch with the highly advanced spirit Ramoth, who is God-oriented. Some channels don't work with the same spirit consistently, and some simply don't know whom they channel. If you choose to work with a channel, remember the words of the Apostle John at the beginning of Chapter 4 of his first letter: "Believe not every spirit, but try the spirits whether they are of God: because many false prophets are gone out into the world. Hereby know ye the spirit of God: Every spirit that confesseth that Jesus Christ is come in the flesh is of God: And every spirit that confesseth not that Jesus Christ is come in the flesh is not of God: and this is that spirit of antichrist." Here is the test: *Are you of God and light? Is Jesus the son of God, and did He walk on earth?* If you don't get positive answers to those questions, you're not dealing with a positive entity, and you need to end the session, surround yourself with light, and get out.

In early fall 2023 I found myself thinking more than usual about the Impressionist painters. I wrote a poem about Renoir's painting "Gypsy Girl" and then became drawn to Monet's beautifully simple "Impression: Sunrise," which centers around a ray of early-morning sunlight playing across a harbor toward us. It reminded me of a similar ray I saw on a lake near sunset more than half a lifetime ago. That made me wonder why there are seemingly meaningless bits of memory that never leave us.

Eventually, I concluded that it's because those bits of memory are part of something larger that we just haven't finished discovering yet—part of a lesson, part of a pattern, maybe just a sliver of a view through a slightly opened doorway that we need to step through. That thinking led to a little logometric poem that I'll leave you with, along with my best wishes, now that I've said what I have to say.

Impression: Sunset

I could not know
how young I was.
Across the lake, sunset
poured a narrow path

toward me, sparkles walking
the lake's quick tips,
brief candles leading west.
I was thirty. Water

inched its heavy way.
I inched mine. Memories
linger, lessons ripening, waiting
for wisdom, somewhere west,

where paths all lead.
I have forgotten more
than many people live;
still, that sunset rides

my steps toward knowing.
Who was with me?
I don't recall. Someone
else on a path.

ALL THINGS PARANORMAL

Investigations, explanations and deliberations on the paranormal, supernatural, explainable or unexplainable. 6th Books seeks to give answers while nourishing the soul: whether making use of the scientific model or anecdotal and fun, but always beautifully written.
Titles cover everything within parapsychology: how to, lifestyles, alternative medicine, beliefs, myths and theories.
If you have enjoyed this book, why not tell other readers by posting a review on your preferred book site?

Recent bestsellers from 6th Books are:

The Scars of Eden
Paul Wallis
How do we distinguish between our ancestors' ideas of God and close encounters of an extraterrestrial kind?
Paperback: 978-1-78904-852-0 ebook: 978-1-78904-853-7

The Afterlife Unveiled
What the dead are telling us about their world!
Stafford Betty
What happens after we die? Spirits speaking through mediums know, and they want us to know.
This book unveils their world...
Paperback: 978-1-84694-496-3 ebook: 978-1-84694-926-5

Harvest: The True Story of Alien Abduction
G.L. Davies
G.L. Davies's most-terrifying investigation yet reveals one woman's terrifying ordeal of alien visitation, nightmarish visions and a prophecy of destruction on a scale never before seen in Pembrokeshire's peaceful history.
Paperback: 978-1-78904-385-3 ebook: 978-1-78904-386-0

Wisdom from the Spirit World
carole j. obley
What can those in spirit teach us about the enduring bond of love, the immense power of forgiveness, discovering our life's purpose and finding peace in a frantic world?
Paperback: 978-1-78904-302-0 ebook: 978-1-78904-303-7

Spirit Release

Sue Allen

A guide to psychic attack, curses, witchcraft, spirit attachment, possession, soul retrieval, haunting, deliverance, exorcism and more, as taught at the College of Psychic Studies.

Paperback: 978-1-84694-033-0 ebook: 978-1-84694-651-6

Advanced Psychic Development

Becky Walsh

Learn how to practise as a professional, contemporary spiritual medium.

Paperback: 978-1-84694-062-0 ebook: 978-1-78099-941-8

Where After

Mariel Forde Clarke

A journey that will compel readers to view life after death in a completely different way.

Paperback: 978-1-78904-617-5 ebook: 978-1-78904-618-2

Poltergeist! A New Investigation into Destructive Haunting

John Fraser

Is the Poltergeist "syndrome" the only type of paranormal phenomena that can really be proven?

Paperback: 978-1-78904-397-6 ebook: 978-1-78904-398-3

A Little Bigfoot: On the Hunt in Sumatra

Pat Spain

Pat Spain lost a layer of skin, pulled leeches off his nether regions, and was violated by an Orangutan for this book.

Paperback: 978-1-78904-605-2 ebook: 978-1-78904-606-9

Astral Projection Made Easy and overcoming the fear of death

Stephanie June Sorrell

From the popular Made Easy series, *Astral Projection Made Easy* helps to eliminate the fear of death through discussion of life beyond the physical body.

Paperback: 978-1-84694-611-0 ebook: 978-1-78099-225-9

Haunted: Horror of Haverfordwest

G.L. Davies

Blissful beginnings for a young couple turn into a nightmare after purchasing their dream home in Wales in 1989.

Paperback: 978-1-78535-843-2 ebook: 978-1-78535-844-9

Readers of ebooks can buy or view any of these bestsellers by clicking on the live link in the title. Most titles are published in paperback and as an ebook. Paperbacks are available in traditional bookshops. Both print and ebook formats are available online.

Find more titles and sign up to our readers' newsletter at **www.6th-books.com**

Join the 6th books Facebook group at **6th Books The world of the Paranormal**